George Washington Carver

George Washington Carver

JAMES MARION GRAY

Silver Burdett Press
Englewood Cliffs, New Jersey

Dedicated to Dr. Austin Wingate Curtis, Jr.

CONSULTANTS:

Jessie B. Gladden
Divisional Specialist
Office of Social Studies
Baltimore City Schools
Baltimore, Maryland

Catherine J. Lenix-Hooker
Deputy Chief
Schomburg Center for Research in Black Culture
New York Public Library
New York City

Acknowledgments and Photograph Acknowledgments are listed on p. 137

SERIES AND COVER DESIGN:
R STUDIO T • Raúl Rodríguez and Rebecca Tachna.
ART DIRECTOR:
Linda Huber
MANAGING EDITOR:
Nancy Furstinger
PROJECT EDITOR:
Richard G. Gallin
PHOTO RESEARCH:
Omni-Photo Communications, Inc.

Published by Silver Burdett Press, Inc., a division of
Simon & Schuster, Inc., Englewood Cliffs, NJ 07632

Library of Congress Cataloging-in-Publication Data

Gray, James Marion.
George Washington Carver / James Marion Gray.
p. cm.—(Pioneers in change)
Includes bibliographical references (p.127).
Summary: Describes the life and accomplishments of the former slave who became a
scientist and devoted his career to helping the South improve its agriculture.
1. Carver, George Washington, 1864?–1943—Juvenile literature.
2. Afro-American agriculturists—Biography—Juvenile literature.
3. Agriculturists—United States—Biography—Juvenile literature.
[1. Carver, George Washington, 1864?–1943. 2. Agriculturists.
3. Afro-Americans—Biography.] I. Title. II. Series.
S417.C3G73 1990
630'.92—dc20
[B]   90-8614
[92]   CIP
                                             AC

Manufactured in the United States of America.
ISBN 0-382-09964-8 [lib. bdg.]
10 9 8 7 6 5 4 3 2 1
ISBN 0-382-09969-0 [pbk.]
10 9 8 7 6 5 4 3 2 1

CONTENTS

1

Beating the Odds

As John Bentley slowly approached on horseback, the hopes of Moses and Susan Carver and Jim were crushed. Their prayers apparently had gone unanswered as the lone rider drew closer to the saddened trio. Mary and her youngest child were surely gone forever.

Finally, as the horse stood towering over the Carvers and Jim, Bentley sadly announced that he had been unable to find Mary. He said there were many rumors regarding her fate. First he had been told that she was dead. Later he was told that she had been seen riding North with some soldiers. Another witness told of her being sent by boat to Louisiana.

The Carvers were devastated by the news. Bentley, however, did have some good news to report. Mary's baby had been found in the company of some women. Apparently the kidnappers had decided the sickly child was not worth keeping and had abandoned him. Bentley, turning around, loosened his coat, which was tied to the back of the saddle. The Carvers and Jim never imagined that the bundle tied to the saddle held Mary's baby, little George!

Neither Bentley nor the Carvers had any reason to suspect a bright future for the sickly child. Yet he would survive and become one of the world's greatest and most beloved scientists, Dr. George Washington Carver. The nurturing love provided by his adoptive parents, affectionately called "Uncle Mose" and "Aunt Sue," helped to mold the child's character. His intellectual ability and personality led to his becoming the most widely recognized African American, with the possible exception of the Reverend Martin Luther King, Jr. This child, separated from his mother and discarded, would be heralded by world leaders, inventors, industrialists, and educators as the Saint Scientist, the Wizard of Tuskegee, the Black (Luther) Burbank, and the Black Leonardo (da Vinci). The personality and achievements of this pioneer in change were shaped by a multitude of forces. Many of those forces surfaced during the first decade of his life.

The Carvers were German immigrants. They had moved to Missouri in about 1838. Earlier, they had lived in Ohio and Illinois. The Preemption Act of 1841 was passed to encourage small farmers to settle in the West. This law enabled anyone who lived on and improved 160 acres of land for six months to purchase it from the United States government for $1.25 per acre. Like many others, Moses Carver was not content to own only 160 acres. As soon as the land was offered for sale, he purchased 240 acres.

Moses selected a good farm site, one having an abundant water supply. Two springs and a creek were located near the family cabin. His acreage included open grassland

and woods. He had ample land for growing crops and a readily available supply of building material and firewood. The original cabin was made of logs. It had one window and a fireplace. The cabin had no floor. In this simple dwelling lived Moses, his wife Susan, and three children taken in by the Carvers following the death of the children's father in 1839.

The years from 1840 to 1860 witnessed tremendous growth in both the economy and population of this part of Missouri. The region proved to be an ideal setting for both crops and livestock production. A crossroads village developed near a diamond-shaped grove of trees located close to the Carver farm. This settlement became known as both Diamond Grove and Diamond. Later, Diamond became the official name of this area as it became a city. In its early days, Diamond Grove consisted of a general store, a combined blacksmith shop and post office, and one church, which served people from several different Christian groups. The church building was used as a school during the week.

As the surrounding region became more densely populated, the value of the Carvers' property increased. In 1860 its listed cash value of three thousand dollars made it the seventh most valued piece of real estate in Marion Township. By that time, Carver was cultivating a hundred acres. His varied crops included corn, wheat, oats, Irish potatoes, hay, and flax. The Carvers also maintained livestock, an orchard, perhaps as many as sixty beehives, and a garden.

As Carver expanded his farming activities, his need for additional help became evident. As long as the three orphaned children remained with the Carvers, they were helpful on the farm. However, one by one they moved away and established their own homes. Moses hired someone to help him in the fields. In 1855, despite his reputed philo-

The bill of sale for George's mother. Moses Carver paid seven hundred dollars for her.

sophical opposition to slavery, Carver purchased a thirteen-year-old girl named Mary to help Susan maintain the house. His distaste for buying another human being was somewhat lessened by his being able to make the purchase directly from a neighbor. The bill of sale for Mary indicates that she was purchased for seven hundred dollars.

While they owned Mary and her children, both Moses and Susan Carver remained committed to their basic opposition to slavery. They also supported the Union as tension over the question of slavery grew before the outbreak of the Civil War.

The fruits of prosperity enabled the Carvers to build a new cabin. Mary and her children moved into the original cabin. Mary was responsible for cooking for the Carvers and helping Susan with other household chores.

It is not known how many children Mary had. There are references to twin girls, who died in infancy. Years later

George made reference to a sister who had been kidnapped along with him and his mother. Mary's only child whose birth date is known was Jim, born in 1859.

Less is known about George's birth date. Various biographers have listed the year of his birth from 1859 to 1865. In his early adulthood, George consistently recalled that he was born "about 1865." At other times, George said that his birth came "near the end of the war" or "just as freedom was declared." He once wrote that he was about two weeks old when the Civil War ended.

The identity of George's father is uncertain. The same is true of Jim's father. George usually referred to his father as being a slave who lived on a neighboring farm. His father was reportedly killed in a log-hauling accident near the time of George's birth.

Before the Civil War the citizens of Missouri were deeply divided in their allegiances. In Missouri, the Civil War was literally fought between brothers. Even members of the Carver clan fought on opposing sides. Located between Unionist Kansas and Confederate Arkansas, southwest Missouri was often the site of bloody battles during the Civil War. The nearby town of Neosho was the county seat of Newton County—that is, the place from which the county was governed. It was occupied at different times by Confederate and Union armies. The Confederates briefly established a rebel government in Neosho. Throughout this period, local residents were victimized by Union raiders, Confederate outlaws called bushwhackers, and roving bands of civilian outlaws.

Being both prosperous and a slaveowner, Moses Carver fell victim to raiders on at least three occasions. During the first raid, the raiders rode onto the Carver farm and demanded money. Carver refused to hand over his money.

The raiders decided that Moses might become more cooperative if they were to hang him by his thumbs from the limbs of an old walnut tree. As he was hanging, evidently in great pain, Moses still refused to cooperate. Finally, in desperation, the gang members took hot coals from a nearby fire and held them to the soles of Moses' bare feet. As the sweat began to run down Moses' face and into his beard, the raiders realized that he was willing to die rather than give in to their demands and tactics. They decided to leave. They and Moses knew a return visit was likely.

On their next visit to the Carvers' farm, the raiders were more successful. As they began to ransack the property, they kicked over several beehives. To their surprise, they learned that the beehives contained something that to them at least was sweeter than honey—Moses' money. After this financial loss, Carver hid his money in many different places throughout his farm.

The raids caused the Carvers to be more alert whenever they heard approaching horses. In addition to his money, Moses knew that night riders might try to steal Mary and her children and sell them. One night Moses' feared nightmare became reality. Alarmed by the sound of running horses, Carver dashed toward Mary's cabin. As he rushed into the cabin, he yelled for Mary to grab her infant son and run. Moses fled the cabin with Jim. Mary and George were not so fortunate. As Mary prepared to flee, she was surrounded by several riders on horseback. Although scared, Mary fiercely held George as one of the riders pulled them onto his horse.

Moses and Jim returned to find the cabin empty.

Mary and her children had become beloved members of the Carver family. Moses wanted Mary and her youngest son to be returned at any cost. A neighbor named John Bentley was in a position to offer his services. As a Union scout

Moses Carver (right), a German immigrant, had lived in Ohio and
Illinois before moving to Missouri.

7

stationed in Neosho, Bentley was familiar with many of the guerrilla groups. He agreed to search for Mary and George. If he located the pair, he would attempt to "steal" them back for Moses. Carver pledged forty acres of his best timberland and Pacer, a thoroughbred racehorse, for the safe return of Mary and George.

Eager to earn the reward, Bentley rode horseback about fifty miles southward into Arkansas. When he returned with only little George to show for his effort, Bentley believed it was unfair to hold Moses responsible for the entire reward. He decided to accept only the racehorse valued at three hundred dollars.

2

Bending the Twig

By the end of 1865, southwest Missouri was experiencing a renewed sense of peace and stability. The war was over. Solutions to both the social and economic turmoil stemming from the Civil War were being sought. The Carvers, like most citizens, were "picking up the pieces" of their shattered lives and looking to the future with a sense of hope.

For George, "Uncle Mose" and "Aunt Sue" became the only parents he could remember. Both George and Jim moved into the Carvers' main cabin. The childless Carvers again assumed the responsibility of raising someone else's children. The two brothers were loved as sons by the Carvers and never mistreated.

As George grew older, he began to ask about his family's background. He was unable to learn very much about his mother. Aunt Sue was never able to discuss Mary without weeping. George often stood by his mother's spinning wheel lost in his thoughts. Mary's spinning wheel and the bill of sale for her purchase later became two of George's most cherished possessions.

Although they were treated as sons by the Carvers, Jim and George were expected to work hard around the farm. Jim was blessed with good health. He was tall and very robust. He was able to do heavy chores around the farm. In the 1880 census, he was listed as being "hired labor" on the Carver farm.

George, in contrast, was frail and sickly. He had suffered from a severe case of whooping cough. As a young child he repeatedly suffered from an inflammation of the voice box and windpipe. His stunted growth during his early childhood and his severely damaged vocal cords may have been the result of his having had both pneumonia and tuberculosis. George later recalled that he could barely talk and could ride "half-fare" until he was in his twenties. Until his death, the high pitch of his voice startled most people who met him for the first time.

George's illnesses often left him physically exhausted. The Carvers therefore would ask him to do the lighter farm work. As his age and size permitted, his assigned tasks included providing water for the farm animals, planting and weeding the garden, picking fruit, and grooming the horses. He also helped Aunt Sue with household chores such as washing clothes and cooking. Because of his frailty and the Carvers' advancing age, George was pampered by the Carvers as if he were their grandson. Once he had completed his chores, he would spend time wandering through the fields and nearby woods. He spent countless hours roaming through the woods, studying everything imaginable. He was as fascinated by rocks and soil samples as he was by the assorted plants, reptiles, birds, and insects found during his daily adventures. He would fill his pockets with his newly acquired specimens, planning to store them inside the cabin.

After some unpleasant encounters with George's frogs and a milkweed pod, which burst open inside the cabin, Susan Carver began to make George empty his pockets before he could go inside. George solved this problem by building a pen for his frogs outside. He piled his rocks outside by the chimney. Occasionally Susan would declare that the rock pile was too large. George would then be forced to select some favorite rocks and discard the others.

Climbing trees, tossing rocks and pebbles, swimming, and fishing were some of George's favorite pastimes. Although George loved to fish throughout his life, the accidental killing of a bird by a tossed stone resulted in his avoiding game hunting. The memory of the small bloodied mass of feathers cupped in his hands haunted George the rest of his life. Even in adulthood, Carver could not endure the sight of blood.

During his early years with the Carvers, George began his lifelong love affair with plants. Most likely around the age of seven or eight George's fascination with plants became evident to the neighbors. They began to refer fondly to George as the "Plant Doctor." George often made "house calls" to examine ailing plants. After making a diagnosis, George would offer advice to the neighbors. His suggested remedies included changing the amount of water or the frequency of watering, altering the amount of sunlight received by the plant, or changing the soil. George would take the most severe "cases" to his secret garden in the woods. In this plot of soil, which measured approximately three feet by six feet, George would treat plants by pruning branches, removing diseased or damaged leaves, and shifting the plants from one soil mixture to another until each plant was thriving. The grateful neighbors shared information about George's success stories with other neighbors. Consequently, George was always in demand. At the same time, he was learning to care for plants through practical, hands-on experience.

George was exposed to the concept of self-sufficiency throughout his years of living with the Carvers. The Carvers' farm was almost completely self-contained. They seldom had to turn to others for help.

Flax and hemp were grown to provide materials for clothing. Using Mary's spinning wheel and a loom, Susan was able to spin yarn and thread and to weave cloth of flax, hemp, and wool. An assortment of tree barks were used as sources of dyes for the cloth. Chestnut bark was used for browns, oak for black, and hickory for yellow. The Carvers also tanned leather and made their shoes. George was taught that nothing should be wasted. Nothing was burned or thrown out if it could be eaten by the farm animals.

Almost the only items that the Carvers needed to buy were coffee and sugar. Even those items were bartered, that is, traded, for other items produced by the Carvers. The extra supplies from the farm were stored for use during the winter. Assorted meats, lard, and butter filled the smokehouse. Sun-dried fruits were stored for the winter. Assorted vegetables were buried in trenches. They were collected and cooked throughout the winter.

Uncle Mose, an expert bee hunter, was always ready to either collect honey or gain another beehive. He would trail bees to their tree. After dark he and Jim would use burning rags and tobacco to "smoke them out" of the tree. Sometimes enough honey to fill a washtub could be removed from a single tree. Uncle Mose would add beehives to his collection by cutting a section of the tree and putting a top on it. Uncle Mose was one of those fortunate individuals who can handle bees and not be stung. He could stick his hand into a tree hole and search among the bees until he had located the large queen. He would then clip her wings to prevent her from flying away with the swarm of bees behind her. George observed these activities from a safe distance.

George learned some valuable lessons as he visited the homes of neighbors. One of his most inspiring lessons was provided during a visit to the Fred Baynham farm. George was standing in the Baynhams' kitchen when his curiosity led him to go into the parlor. The large family portraits hanging on the parlor wall were the first paintings George had ever seen. When it was explained to him that an "artist" had made the paintings through the use of his hands, George decided he could do likewise.

George was never the same after that visit to the Baynhams' parlor. From that day until the day he died, George was an artist. Any type of surface was viewed as a possible canvas. He was constantly scratching images on rocks, boards, and the ground. Berries, roots, and barks became the sources of his paints. An old can or a piece of broken glass was often decorated by his artwork.

Throughout his life George was known for his concern for others. A profound event in George's life occurred in connection with his concern for a young neighbor boy. Using one of Moses Carver's knives, George whittled a pair of crutches for this crippled child. Afterward, George wished he owned a knife. Then one night George had a dream. In the dream, he saw a watermelon lying in a cornfield. The watermelon had been cut and partially eaten. Part of the watermelon rind was lying at the base of three cornstalks. Near the rind, a small black knife with two blades could be seen.

After awakening the next morning, George hurriedly ate his breakfast. He then dashed across the fields to the place seen in his dream. He found the knife just as it had appeared in the dream. He enjoyed telling this story throughout his life. The small black knife became one of his dearest treasures. George went through life believing in Divine Revelation. His openness in discussing such revelations was characteristic of both his private and public images.

George received his early religious instruction while attending Sunday services at the Little Locust Grove Church. The church was located about one mile from the Carver farm. As George and Jim listened to the sermons, they were exposed to a wide range of religious views. That was because the church had circuit ministers from several different religious groups, including Methodist, Baptist, Disciples of Christ, and Presbyterian. Circuit ministers traveled from one church to another throughout the year and so served many small communities. The two brothers gained a wealth of religious doctrine while attending the church services. They also learned to be tolerant of different religious views. Throughout his life, George made it a practice to attend church services wherever he went—but the church services did not have to be of only a specific religious group. To him, every church represented a place to honor God.

George and Jim enjoyed the local church services so much that they decided to enroll in the school held in the same building. The boys were admitted to the school but were forced to withdraw almost immediately because they were African Americans. This was the brothers' first encounter with racial prejudice.

In 1865 the new state constitution in Missouri provided for free schooling for blacks, but not for whites. Each township was required to provide a school if it had more than twenty black citizens between the ages of five and twenty. Marion Township did not have the required number of eligible blacks. In some situations, black children were permitted to attend the local schools for white children. Sometimes local whites were successful in having the admitted blacks withdrawn. Apparently, such was the situation in the withdrawal of George and Jim from the local school.

George was especially disappointed by being unable to attend school. He knew the Carvers had taught him everything they knew. Yet he wanted to learn so much more. In his later years, George described the frustrations he felt as he sought to learn more in Diamond Grove:

> When just a mere tot...my very soul thirsted for an education. I literally lived in the woods. I wanted to know every strange stone, flower, insect, bird, or beast. No one could tell me. My only book was an old Webster's Elementary Spelling Book. I would seek the answer here without satisfaction. I almost knew the book by heart.

The arrival of Steven Slane in 1876 provided George with the hope of gaining more of an education. After this young educated man arrived in Diamond Grove, he offered to become a private tutor for George. But the student surpassed his teacher. George began searching for another source of information. The only answer seemed to be one requiring a major change in George's life—leaving the Carvers and moving to Neosho.

The Carvers realized George was special and needed an opportunity to attend school. They agreed with his decision to leave home. He could enroll in the free school for blacks in Neosho, located about eight miles south of Diamond Grove.

When George left the Carver farm around 1877, he was about twelve. Although he would visit the Carvers on the weekends, he would never live with them again. Susan and Moses Carver were great contributors to George's personal outlook. Susan was the source of many of George's skills— sewing, cooking, laundering, and needlework. Moses inspired George's love for music, his tendency not to be wasteful, and his willingness to be different in the face of criticism. At this time, George lacked a formal education. Yet he was highly educated regarding many practical aspects of life. His loving foster parents, the Carvers, his beloved brother, Jim, his many caring neighbors, and the creatures of nature had contributed many first-rate lessons for George. The words of the eighteenth-century English poet Alexander Pope can be used to describe young George as he began his long walk toward Neosho:

'Tis education forms the common
mind: Just as the twig is bent
the tree's inclined.

3

Hope and Despair

The road leading to Neosho was familiar to George. He and Jim had on occasion visited the county seat with Uncle Mose. Those trips had been exciting and always included round-trip transportation. This day's trip was strikingly different. He was walking alone to a place where he'd live among strangers.

With his possessions tied in a large bandanna, George reached Neosho by late afternoon. He spent the remaining hours of daylight roaming around town trying to decide his next move. Nightfall found the weary traveler standing before an open barn door. Realizing the barn offered shelter for the night, George went inside. The hayloft became his bed. His sleep was disturbed during the night as the restless horses moved about in their stalls and hungry mice and rats scurried through the hay.

At dawn, George slipped out of the barn. After walking

around for a while, he decided to sit on a woodpile. He had barely sat down when a small African-American woman walked out of her nearby house and headed for the woodpile. As her eyes met George's she realized he was hungry. Mariah and Andrew Watkins soon had a breakfast guest. After treating George to a hearty breakfast, Mrs. Watkins gave him another surprise—a thorough scrubbing with soap and water. As a midwife, one having delivered hundreds of babies, Mariah Watkins insisted on personal cleanliness. After being bathed, George was wrapped in a large apron and instructed in performing some household chores.

The childless couple were immediately impressed by George's personality and invited him to live with them. "Aunt Mariah" and "Uncle Andy" were now his new foster parents. Under the supervision of Aunt Mariah, George became an expert launderer. He enjoyed ironing clothes to perfection. Scrubbing the floors and applying whitewash to the walls were other chores cheerfully carried out by the new family member.

Aunt Mariah was a devout Christian. She and George attended the local African Methodist Church. The minister made a great impression on George as he observed this church leader living such a devout life. The minister was unable to read. Each Sunday a member of the congregation would take the Bible and read a passage aloud before the congregation. Once the Scriptures were read for the benefit of the congregation the minister would begin his sermon— giving his interpretation of the passage and its relevance to life and spiritual growth.

George's own religious growth was also aided by Aunt Mariah. In church, she was not ashamed to become emotionally caught up by the preaching and singing. At home with George, she taught him to love the Word of God. Many

Mariah Watkins had a strong religious influence on George Washington Carver's life.

decades later, as he approached eighty, he was still reading from the Bible given to him by Aunt Mariah. The bookmark used as he read the Bible was the same one he had embroidered as this beloved guardian watched.

With the Watkins couple George found love and security in a new community. At the same time, the reason for his moving to Neosho was satisfied by an unlikely circumstance. The small school for the African Americans in Neosho was located next to the Watkinses' house. A fence separated the two properties. By the time of George's arrival, Lincoln School's first teacher, a white woman, had been replaced by a young black male, Stephen A. Frost. His seventy-five students were crowded into a classroom measuring fourteen feet by sixteen feet.

George was quickly accepted by his classmates. And he gained a surname. Following the tradition of former slaves, the boy known in Diamond Grove as the Carvers' George was renamed George Carver. At recess, George would jump the fence. With a book in hand, he would dash home. While doing the laundry, he would read the book that he had propped against a wall. When George heard the bell ending recess, he would rush back to the classroom. During the evenings, George would complete his chores and then study.

George and his classmates were soon joined by Jim Carver. Jim, lonely for his brother and curious about receiving an education, had traveled to Neosho. Jim did not enjoy reading books and studying. He soon left school and became a local plasterer.

George continued to attend class at Lincoln School; however, he began to dislike Stephen Frost. George was very upset by his teacher's marriage to the woman with whom Jim had fallen in love. George was also resentful of his teacher's embarrassment at being African American.

Even though he was good at playing mumblety-peg and marbles, George preferred work to play. He felt a great need to be earning a living rather than seemingly wasting time with games. George was always seeking jobs to fill his free time. A local couple named Slater offered him a job doing household chores. Mrs. Slater trusted George so much that on one occasion she left him in charge of the house while she and her husband traveled to St. Louis. When the Slaters stayed away longer than expected, George began to do as much cleaning and repair work as possible. When the Slaters returned, George began to list everything he had accomplished while they were away. Mrs. Slater stopped George as he continued to brag. "Now, George, don't tell me the number of things you have done, but how well you have done them." Mrs. Slater's friendly advice remained with George throughout his life.

George was always learning how to do something new. As he observed individuals making something with their hands, he would think to himself that he could do the same thing. Such was the case whenever he watched Aunt Mariah busily working with her handicrafts. George was fascinated by her expertise in sewing, knitting, plaiting rugs, and crocheting. Once he mastered these skills, he loved doing them until the time of his death.

At school George soon realized that he had learned everything Stephen Frost could teach him. That realization, together with his long-term poor health, caused George to ponder leaving Neosho. Perhaps a "change in scenery" would be good.

The opportunity to move on presented itself to George in the late 1870s. A local family decided to move to Fort Scott, Kansas. They agreed to permit George to ride with them. As a parting token of affection, Uncle Andy made a will leaving everything he owned to George. At the same time, George humorously agreed to leave to Uncle Andy all the pennies he might save in life. Before George began the ride westward, he and Jim walked to Diamond Grove for a final visit with the Carvers.

Back in Neosho, George and Jim were separated again as George climbed onto one of the two mule-drawn wagons. The wagons were overloaded with furniture, cookware, clothing, and passengers. To lighten the load, George and the family members had to take turns walking during the trip. Several days later, after traveling about seventy-five miles, the group arrived in Fort Scott.

Upon arriving in Fort Scott, George began to look for a job. When he heard that the Felix Payne family was looking for a household helper, he went there immediately. When Mrs. Payne asked George if he knew how to cook he replied, "Yes, Ma'am." George was then told just how demanding Mr. Payne was about his meals. If the meal didn't meet his expectations, he would refuse to eat. With that warning, Mrs. Payne told George what he should cook for dinner.

George had no idea about how to prepare the named dishes. Being a quick thinker, George explained that he wanted to prepare the dishes just as Mr. Payne would prefer. He then asked Mrs. Payne to show him how to do so. As she was showing George how to prepare each item on the menu, she didn't realize how George was succeeding with his plan. As George learned how to prepare each dish, he surpassed Mrs. Payne's expertise in cooking. He became such an outstanding cook that he won a local cooking contest with his entries of yeast bread, salt-rising bread, and yeast and buttermilk batter biscuits.

Overall, George had a rough time in Fort Scott. He would save enough money to enroll in school for a week or two. When he was financially broke, he would temporarily withdraw from school until he could afford to return.

On the night of March 26, 1879, George's plans to live in Fort Scott were dramatically changed. Earlier that day a black man accused of raping a twelve-year-old white girl had been found in an abandoned coal mine. He was taken to the county jail in Fort Scott. Throughout the afternoon and evening, a crowd of about one thousand whites began forming. After sundown, the crowd watched as about thirty masked men forced their way into the jail and dragged the prisoner into the street. What then took place was one of the several thousand lynchings that took place in the United States in the several decades after the Civil War. George witnessed the hanging and mutilation of the prisoner. The final indignity to the corpse involved pouring oil on the body and setting it afire. By this time, the frenzied crowd was gleefully cheering on the vigilantes. George realized the crowd was bent on racial revenge. As the stench of burning flesh filled the night air, George feared for his own life. By sunrise, George had fled from Fort Scott. He would never return.

4

A Closed Door

After fleeing from Fort Scott, George became a wanderer. He traveled throughout Kansas working at many different jobs. In some communities, George was able to find a job in a greenhouse. He was so happy when he could work with plants. He would even work for free in a greenhouse if a paying job was unavailable.

During his wanderings, George was always squeezing in some formal education. The schools varied greatly from town to town. Whether the school was integrated or segregated, George was content with the opportunity to learn. Year after year, George learned enough to gradually be promoted from one grade to another.

George was always proving himself to be a survivor among strangers. He realized life was not always fair or just. However, he refused to give in to self-pity. Instead, he focused on paths leading to self-improvement.

Carver developed a rarely seen work ethic. He believed he had to completely earn his living. He would not accept more pay than what he thought the job was worth. If he performed a task and was offered a dime when he thought he should only receive a nickel, he would refuse the extra money. To him, accepting extra compensation was illogical. This value system led Carver to give gifts in appreciation of kindness shown to him. Throughout his wanderings, he left a trail of gifts. The gifts were often items that he himself had made.

Carver's way of life often resulted in his becoming lonely. He bought an accordion to relieve his loneliness as he either walked along a road or sat in his room. He spent seven dollars for the instrument. In one town, he was sitting by an open window in his upstairs room when he spotted a music teacher approaching. Hoping to get the teacher's attention and approval, Carver enthusiastically played his accordion. Soon the teacher was standing beneath the open window. Carver eventually noticed the teacher was shaking his head in utter disgust over Carver's poor playing. The aspiring musician slowly stopped playing his instrument. As he took the accordion from his lap and placed it on the floor, he silently vowed not to play it for others to hear until he learned to play it properly.

Soon after arriving in Olathe, Kansas, Carver began to live with a barber, Jerry Johnson, and his wife. He began to attend a school with approximately forty other students. The school building had been a grocery store. When the Johnsons moved, Carver moved in with Christopher and Lucy Seymour. (Mr. Seymour has also been identified as Ben.) The Seymours, like the Watkinses, were childless. They, too, were impressed by Carver. They treated him as if he were a son.

The Seymours played an important role in helping to mold George's ever-deepening respect for both thrift and religion. "Aunt Lucy," an African American formerly owned by a prominent Virginia family, was proud of her social background. She tended to look down on African Americans who lacked her level of refinement. However, she immediately accepted Carver as her social equal. Carver spent many evenings playing with her nieces and nephews. Checkers, tiddlywinks, and dominoes were some of their favorite games.

"Uncle Chris" became a powerful role model for Carver. In his previous living situations, Carver was introduced to religious teachings by the women in the family. With Uncle Chris, George saw that religion could play an important role in the lives of men. He and Uncle Chris attended both morning and afternoon services on Sundays at the local Presbyterian church.

While living with the Seymours, Carver was able to attend school on a more regular basis. He was able to complete both the fifth and sixth grades. During this period, he also became an expert accordion player. Every Friday his classmates were treated to his playing the instrument.

After living in Olathe for about a year, the Seymours moved to Minneapolis, Kansas. Carver moved in with another family in nearby Paola. During the summer of 1880, Carver moved to Minneapolis. By this time, Carver was no longer small. He now stood at least six feet tall.

In Minneapolis, Carver again lived for some time with the Seymours. He helped Aunt Lucy with her laundry business. However, he soon decided to open his own. He believed the town's citizens would support two laundries.

After opening his laundry in a small house, Carver decided to buy the property. The owner agreed to sell.

*This picture was taken in a photographer's studio when George
Carver was about fifteen years old.*

Carver negotiated to buy the property by paying a monthly fee of five dollars. The owner agreed that Carver did not have to worry about having the total amount available on the due date. While he was not always able to meet the due date, Carver worked hard to pay as soon as possible.

Within a year, the town of Minneapolis had experienced tremendous growth. Carver realized his property had increased in value. The previous owner asked Carver about selling the property back to him.

When Carver repeatedly refused to sell the property, the previous owner forced him to sell it. He had told Carver not to worry about late payments. But the contract had actually called for payments on the first day of each month. The previous owner declared that Carver had not kept the agreement since he had made late payments. Even though Carver was disappointed, he knew he had to relocate. This bitter disappointment taught Carver the importance of getting everything in writing.

Throughout his years of traveling in Missouri and Kansas, Carver had made many friends. He enjoyed keeping in touch with those friends by letter. When Carver failed to receive responses to his letters, he became depressed. Then one day Carver was told that another George Carver lived in Minneapolis. This man was receiving the mail intended for Carver. To distinguish himself from this other George Carver, he selected *W* as his middle initial. Later, when someone asked Carver if the *W* stood for "Washington," he simply replied, "Why not?" Although he became known as George Washington Carver, throughout his life he simply signed his name either as George W. Carver or G. W. Carver.

Carver often lacked enough money to buy postage stamps. That meant that he was often unable to respond quickly to those who wrote to him. His brother, Jim Carver, was a reluctant letter writer by nature. The two brothers often lost contact with each other. In 1884, after George had failed to hear from Jim in over a year, he received some sad news. Lucy Seymour went to visit George. She told him that she had heard Jim had died during a smallpox epidemic a year earlier. He had been buried in Seneca, Kansas, located a few miles southwest of Neosho. With the death of Jim, Carver realized he had no living relatives. Now he was truly alone.

For the most part Carver enjoyed the four years he lived in Minneapolis. He was busy with his laundry business. He also did odd jobs throughout the community. One of his closest friends was Dr. James McHenry. The two were introduced by Lucy Seymour, who spent some time working for Dr. McHenry as a nursing assistant. McHenry appreciated Carver's interest in education and loaned him books to read. Those books provided Carver with an even greater desire to continue his education.

In Minneapolis, Carver attended a four-room, two-story school. His white classmates were impressed by his knowledge of history and other subjects. His teacher, Helen Hacker, was very supportive of Carver. When he moved away he presented this beloved teacher with a gold pin as a token of his appreciation.

The population of Minneapolis was predominantly white. Carver became close friends with many of them. One of his dearest friends was classmate Chester Rarig. He was often invited to join the Rarigs for Sunday dinner. Carver was very active in church activities. He also spent hours studying plants, painting, and crocheting.

In January 1884 Carver purchased two lots in Minneapolis for a hundred dollars. In the fall of the same year, he sold the property for five hundred dollars and moved to

Kansas City. He soon found a job as a clerk at the Union Depot, the train station. He also purchased a typewriter and began to learn typing.

While in Kansas City, Carver was able to visit with his former classmate Chester Rarig. Rarig had moved to Kansas City and opened a school of business. One day the two friends entered a restaurant for breakfast. As they sat at the long counter, a waitress approached the pair. She told Rarig that he could be served but not his African-American friend. Rarig was outraged. He and Carver left without ordering. Outside the restaurant, Carver urged his friend to go back and eat and not to worry about him. This scenario would be repeated throughout Carver's life. Yet, each time he was embarrassed more for his white companions than for himself.

Now in his early twenties, Carver decided to enroll in college. He applied by mail to Highland College, a small college in Highland, Kansas. This community is located near the intersection of the borders of Kansas, Nebraska, and Missouri. Highland College, established and supported by the Presbyterian church, had fewer than a hundred male and female students. George was notified of his acceptance and looked forward to his enrolling with great enthusiasm and pride.

During the summer before going to Highland, Carver attended the business school established by Chester Rarig. He took classes in both typing and shorthand. When Carver finished the summer business classes, he decided to spend a few weeks visiting those dear friends from his early childhood.

Before going to Diamond Grove, Carver traveled to Seneca to visit Jim's grave. Afterward he visited with both Moses and Susan Carver. He also attended church services at the Locust Grove Church. George spent the evening among many of his old classmates from Neosho. He played both the accordion and harmonica as his friends sang. Many of the songs were spirituals—religious songs of a deeply emotional character that developed especially among African Americans in the South. Among those spirituals were such favorites as "Tenting on the Old Camp-Ground" and "Swing Low, Sweet Chariot." The joyous reunion was closed by prayer. One of the fathers reminded George that a person could always earn money and lose it, but no one could ever take away a person's education.

As Carver set out for Highland, he made a brief visit to Olathe. There his friends were amazed at his height. They also expressed how happy they were about his decision to attend Highland College.

Carver was bursting with pride and joy when he arrived at Highland. Those feelings, however, were short lived. Carver entered the office of the principal to introduce himself. He saw the Reverend Duncan Brown sitting behind his desk. Without standing, the principal curtly asked, "Well, what do you want?" Carver answered, "I'm George W. Carver, Sir. I've come to matriculate [enroll]." Brown's reply crushed Carver. He was told blacks were not permitted to enroll at Highland. Carver was devastated. No question about his race had been on the application.

As the door to Highland College closed behind him, Carver had the urge to flee from the town as he had years before from Fort Scott. He had fled for his life from Fort Scott. Now, he would be fleeing from the pain of rejection. But this time he could not leave town right away. He was broke and hungry. Earning some money was his first concern.

Word of Carver's rejection by Highland College officials

spread throughout the community. The townspeople were quick to offer job opportunities. Carver was hired by Mrs. John Beeler to help her with household chores. The Beelers owned a large fruit farm near town. In addition to helping the Beelers, George became very active in local church socials.

Although he had been accepted by the townspeople of Highland, George was painfully aware of his inability to attend the local college. He knew that as long as he remained in town, the memories of his rejection would be foremost in his thoughts. Carver decided to head for the western plains of Kansas.

5

Heeding a Friend's Advice

When the United States government opened the western plains of Kansas for settlement in 1878, many
settlers headed West. The first land rush in the area was
followed by another surge of new settlers in 1886. Frank
Beeler was among the second wave of settlers. He was about
the same age as Carver. Beeler had moved from his parents'
farm in Highland to Ness County. On the plains of Ness
County, Beeler built a store. The area around the store
became known as Beeler. Carver followed Frank Beeler to
Ness County in the summer of 1886.

The Homestead Act of 1862 enabled a settler to file a
claim at the nearest land office for 160 acres of land (called a
quarter section) held by the government. After living on the
land for five years, the settler could obtain full title to and
ownership of the land by paying a twenty-four dollar filing
fee. The property often passed from one settler to another

before the final claim was filed. In August 1886, Carver purchased a quarter section of land. The previous owner had given up his claim to the property. Carver's land was located south of Beeler.

While waiting to build his house and plant crops, Carver was hired by the owners of the adjoining Gregg-Steeley Livestock Ranch. He was hired to be of assistance to Mrs. Steeley's son, George H. Steeley. At first Carver was humiliated by Mrs. Steeley's refusal to permit him to eat with her and her son. Later Mrs. Steeley, who was only visiting her son, returned to her home. Carver and Steeley became very good friends. They ate together and spent hours sharing tales. Carver could not have hoped to find a better friend.

Steeley taught Carver how to construct sod houses, including one for himself. (The sod, or grass-covered earth, was cut into bricklike slices for building houses on the prairie.) Carver worked at Steeley's ranch during the day, but spent the night on his own property. This was done in order to meet the legal requirements of maintaining his homestead claim. Carver and Steeley worked together constructing barns, tool sheds, and poultry houses from sod. Carver enjoyed experimenting with sod construction. Carver became known as the best sod builder in Ness County. He completed his home in April 1887. Days later he moved in. His household furnishings included a cookstove, bed, cupboard, table and chairs, and laundry equipment. Carver kept his sod house, which measured fourteen square feet, spotless. Light passing through a window allowed him to keep the interior decorated with plants. Unfortunately, Carver's attempts to dig a well on his property were unsuccessful. He had to carry water from a freshwater spring on Steeley's property three-quarters of a mile away.

Carver cultivated seventeen acres of land, planting corn and vegetables. He also had several chickens. Farming proved to be very difficult on the prairie. In the spring the area was green with vegetation. Newcomers were always successful in growing crops during the spring. They would laugh at the old-timers who told of their own crop failures. Their laughing didn't last long. Soon periods of hot winds, scorching the land, were accompanied by dust storms. Corn, standing lush and green at midmorning, could be reduced to dried, brown stalks by evening.

In mid-January 1888 Carver witnessed the treachery of a winter blizzard. George Steeley was going away for a week. He was going to Larned to buy supplies. The day he left it was a bright, sunny, bitterly cold day. Carver was told to put the livestock in the barn each night in case a blizzard developed. Steeley advised Carver not to go outside for any reason once the livestock had been sheltered. Carver scoffed at the warning. He had seen blizzards before. He resented Steeley's fatherly advice.

Two days later Carver noticed a small bluish cloud. It was two o'clock. By four o'clock he had herded the livestock into the barn. Thirty minutes later, looking through a window, he could not see the barn less than a hundred yards away. Standing in the doorway, he could not see his hand held six inches in front of his face. While holding the rope as a lifeline, he stepped outside. After three or four steps, he turned around. The house was completely hidden by the snow. Individuals caught outside under these conditions could become completely lost. After such prairie blizzards individuals were sometimes found frozen to death within a few feet of safety. When Steeley returned, Carver told him about the ordeal. And he humbly admitted that until then he had only thought that he had seen a real blizzard.

Despite such violent weather, Carver enjoyed living on the prairie. He and his neighbors often spent the evenings playing music. Frank Beeler wrote later, "I look back with a great deal of satisfaction to the concerts we pulled off in the sod houses and also in my store after business hours. Those were the days of real joy." Carver was fascinated by the area and spent countless hours looking for rocks, plants, and Native American relics.

Carver was recognized as one of the most highly educated people in the area. He played his accordion at the local dances and became a member of the Ness County Literary Society. This group met weekly for plays, music, and debates. Carver took his first art lessons from Clara Duncan, an African-American woman. She had moved to Ness County from Talladega, Alabama. In Talladega, located east of Birmingham, she had taught at Talladega College. This was one of the first colleges set up for African Americans.

In June 1888 Carver became restless and decided to move from Ness County. He borrowed three hundred dollars, using his land as collateral, property the lender could keep if Carver failed to repay the loan. Carver used two hundred dollars to pay for his property and to get the title to the land. Shortly after securing the title, Carver left Ness County. Records show that in 1891, apparently unable to repay the loan, Carver deeded the land to his creditor.

As Carver left Ness County, he took with him several specimens of cacti. He valued them more than the clothes he left behind. He was hoping to open a greenhouse some-where down the road. In the meantime, as he traveled from town to town, he used his limited funds to open a temporary laundry business. In each town, he could go into business for about fifty cents. He could buy a washboard for fifteen cents and a tub for a quarter. When he had spent the remaining money for soap, he was in business.

Sometime between 1888 and 1890, Carver reached Winterset, Iowa, located near Des Moines. He was hired as a chef and food buyer by the owner of a local hotel. The positions had become available when the owner's son left to pursue a musical career. Carver proved to be a thrifty food buyer. He reduced the hotel's food expenses by half while maintaining a high-quality food service.

One Sunday morning Carver attended services at the local Methodist church. As he sat near the rear of the church, he was greatly impressed by the soprano voice of the choir leader, Helen Milholland. Carver didn't realize Mrs. Milholland was equally impressed by his tenor voice, which stood out distinctly among the other singers' voices.

The following afternoon, Carver was summoned from the hotel kitchen. He was warmly greeted by Dr. John Milholland. He told Carver that his wife, Helen Milholland, was impressed by Carver's singing talent. She had asked her husband to invite Carver to visit their home. Carver was thrilled by the invitation.

When Carver arrived at the Milholland home, he was pleasantly surprised to learn of the common interests he shared with Mrs. Milholland. She had a greenhouse and loved to paint. As they discussed their interests, Helen suggested that George visit her daily after work. She would give him singing lessons. He could return the favor by giving her art lessons. The Milholland home soon became a second home for Carver.

Unfortunately, the unexpected return of the hotel owner's son left Carver unemployed. Again Carver turned to his life-saving career—that of operating a laundry. He located his business in a cottage near the edge of town. He secured a fifty-dollar loan for equipment. Dr. Milholland was used as a reference to obtain the loan.

One day a friend of the Milhollands noticed Carver crocheting. When she expressed an interest in his work, he showed her a box containing his crocheted lace. She was amazed by the collection of beautiful lace. When she asked Carver what he planned to do with the lace, he replied, "I'm going South to my people later on and I expect to use them in teaching in the schools there."

Carver's laundry was located near the woods. That location made it easy for him to spend hours collecting plant specimens. He began to use the knowledge he had gained in libraries to identify and classify the specimens, that is, to place them in related groups.

Helen Milholland became concerned that Carver's talents would never reach their full potential unless he received more formal education. She was constantly saying, "Now, George, you've got to go back to school. You ought to be in school." George would respond by saying that he couldn't go because he had to work to pay back his loan. Yet Milholland's words would ring in his ears. "You ought to go back to school. George, you know you ought to be in school."

During the summer of 1890, Carver began to avoid Milholland. He simply could not stand the pressure she was placing on him to go to school. Concerned about Carver's well-being, Helen Milholland sent her children to check on him.

Near the end of July, as he was busy ironing, Carver began to argue with himself. He was mentally struggling with Helen Milholland's advice. "You'd better go back to school." "No, I can't go to school." Carver, lost in his thoughts, walked away from the ironing board. Standing before an open window, he heard his voice saying, "Well, then, I will go back to school."

From that moment, Carver felt the burden of going back to school lifting from his shoulders. With a renewed sense of direction, he began to work extra hard to pay off his debt. By fall, he had done so.

Carver gave his artwork to Helen Milholland. And with the profit made from the selling of his possessions, he met his tuition costs for enrolling at Simpson College, located in Indianola, Iowa.

6

Torn Between Two Loves

Carver walked the twenty-five miles from Winterset to Indianola in September 1890. Simpson College, organized under the sponsorship of the Des Moines Conference of the Methodist Episcopal Church, had an enrollment of about three hundred students. It had a faculty of seventeen. Its three buildings provided space for classrooms, offices, and a women's dormitory.

As Carver went to enroll, he didn't know what type of reception he would receive from the administrators or students. He was quite relieved when he was permitted to enroll. The passing students simply stared briefly and then seemed to ignore the newcomer.

Noticing his rather unusual educational background, the administrators asked Carver to enroll in the preparatory school. This was done to make sure he had the necessary background for success in college. He was enrolled in arithmetic, grammar, essays, and etymology—the study of words and their origins. However, he was denied permission to register in the art class. It was assumed that an African American had no practical reason for "wasting" time in such a class. He should take classes to prepare him for a job. Who had ever heard of an African-American artist?

Nevertheless, Carver was determined to study art. He at least wanted the opportunity to try to prove his artistic ability. He finally approached the art director, Etta M. Budd. She was not enthusiastic about admitting Carver to an art class. Carver was given a two-week period to attend the art class. At the end of this period, Budd would evaluate his talent and decide if he could remain in the class. Carver accepted Budd's terms.

Carver's next problem was finding a place to live. The female students lived in the Ladies' Hall dormitory. The male students paid to live in private homes throughout Indianola. Carver was hurting financially. Simpson's president, Dr. Edmund M. Holmes, gave Carver permission to live in an abandoned shack located near the college. Dr. Holmes told Carver that he would urge the other students to hire Carver to do their laundry.

With a place to live and the promise of some income, Carver's next concern was food. After he had paid his tuition, Carver was left with ten cents. At a local meat market he bought a nickel's worth of beef suet, hard fat. He spent the other nickel on cornmeal.

Unfortunately, Dr. Holmes forgot to mention Carver's laundry business to the student body. Each day Carver's food supply diminished. And his income remained at zero.

Carver was concerned about his financial woes. Yet, his main concern was his staying in Budd's art class. At the end of two weeks, Budd made no comment to Carver. When he could no longer tolerate the suspense, Carver approached his teacher. "Miss Budd, you said that if I showed any special talent I could stay in the class. May I?" Carver's anxiety disappeared as Budd said, "I don't see why not. You may start doing landscapes."

A few days later Budd went to visit one of her former students, Mrs. Sophia E. Liston. She told Liston about a needy student who had volunteered to cut her stovewood to pay his tuition. Budd urged Liston to find him a room.

Liston decided at once to visit Carver and offer assistance. However, when Carver answered her knock at the door of his shack, Liston was so touched emotionally that she couldn't state the reason for her visit. She quickly thought of a way to help Carver without embarrassing him. She told Carver that she had been told about his artistic talent. She was wondering if he would be willing to help her improve her artistic techniques.

Carver offered his help without hesitation. Liston now saw how she could tactfully offer to help Carver. She pointed out that it would be more convenient for both of them if Carver lived closer to Simpson College. She gave Carver the address of some dear friends who had an available room.

Liston lost no time in spreading the word about Carver's financial problems. His laundry business became a booming success. Carver made his furniture from wooden crates donated by local store owners. Then one afternoon, following his classes, Carver opened his door to discover some new furniture. In an undated letter to the Milhollands, Carver wrote, "The people are very kind to me here and the students are wonderfully good[. They] took into their heads that I was working too hard and had not home comforts eneough [enough] and they clubbed together and bought me three real nice chairs and a very nice table[. They] left them for me while I was at school." This is a good example of Carver's writing style. He paid very little attention to grammar, punctuation, and sentence structure. Yet he was aware of his shortcomings in written communication. On one occasion he wrote to a friend, "I am glad that you can read my letters. I was not aware that my spelling and grammar were even respectable."

Carver was never able to identify which students had actually given him the furniture. His classmates knew he would not knowingly accept charity. Yet they wanted to help him. And they did. They would cautiously slip free tickets to local events or a half dollar under his door when they knew he was away.

Although Carver may have been ignored when he first enrolled, he became a very popular student at Simpson College. Many of his classmates enjoyed visiting him at home. They also enjoyed joining him for his long walks through the woods on Saturday and Sunday afternoons. He joined the college's baseball team. He also joined one of the literary societies and provided music for local concerts.

Carver was especially fond of Etta Budd. In a letter to the Milhollands, Carver wrote, "My teacher told me the other day that she is sorry she did not find me out sooner, so she could have planned differently for me." In a 1922 biographical sketch, Carver noted that he was indebted to Etta Budd for his successes. He added, "Miss Budd helped me in whatever way she could; often going far out of her way to encourage and see that I had such things as I needed."

Once Budd had given Carver permission to remain in her class and paint landscapes, he did so without questioning her. He continued doing landscapes even though he was not fond of them. One evening Budd left her classroom to go out for dinner. Carver and another student remained in class working on their projects. As she tried to paint some red roses, the other student became so frustrated that she threw her brush. Carver offered to help her.

George was busily painting the roses when the teacher was heard entering the building. Alice, the other student, screamed in a panic. George was so startled that he knocked over a statue. Budd was understandably upset when she entered the classroom. While scolding Carver for breaking the statue, she noticed the red roses on the canvas. "Why Alice, that's the best work I've seen you do. I really believe you've caught the spirit at last!"

George and Alice grinned at each other. Then loud laughter filled the room. Finally, regaining her composure, Alice confessed, "It isn't mine. George did it." Budd turned to Carver, "Why didn't you tell me you could do flowers like this? I've a good notion to give you a Scotch blessing [spanking]! Go get another canvas and start a still life!"

George immediately became an independent art student. Budd allowed him to paint anything he wished.

George's two great loves, nature and art, began to present a problem for him. How could the two areas of interest be combined in one career—one providing a means of adequate income? His beloved teacher Etta Budd began to ponder the same question. She knew that artists were not well paid. She wanted Carver to earn a respectable income through a practical career. Yet she knew that in order to be both financially successful and emotionally content, Carver should pursue a career along the line of his natural talents.

Budd had noticed Carver's interest in plants. He often brought plants to class. She had seen the plants resulting from his experiments with cross-pollination—placing pollen from one flower into a different type of flower—and grafting, the transferring of cut plant parts from one plant to

George Washington Carver devoted some of his time in college to painting.

another. She came to believe that Carver should pursue a career in botany, the study of plants.

Eventually, Budd was able to convince Carver to enroll at Iowa State, the agricultural college located in Ames. She was familiar with the curriculum, and she was well acquainted with at least one member of the faculty. Her father, Joseph Lancaster Budd, was a professor of horticulture—the science of growing fruits, vegetables, and flowers—at Iowa State.

7

Preparing for a Calling

Professor Joseph L. Budd was expecting George Carver and greeted him as he arrived on campus. After extending a warm welcome to Carver, he directed him to the dining hall. But racial bigotry awaited Carver. In the dining hall, he was told that he could not eat with the white students. He would have to eat in the basement with the hired field workers.

Carver wrote to his friend Mrs. Liston for advice. As soon as she received his letter, she boarded a train for Ames. She and Carver spent the day touring the campus, visiting the various buildings. At mealtime, she would enter the dining hall with Carver and then follow him to the basement for their meal. As Liston accompanied Carver throughout the day, the students took notice. That day marked Carver's last day of social isolation at Iowa State.

Earlier, Etta Budd had contacted Dr. Louis H. Pammel, professor of botany. She asked Dr. Pammel to help find

Carver a job. He honored her request. Carver was hired as a janitor in North Hall. He was also provided living quarters in Dr. Pammel's office on the first floor of North Hall. Dr. Pammel then relocated his office to the second floor.

Although having to go to the dining hall basement may have caused Carver to wonder about his future treatment at Iowa State, his fears were short-lived. Later, he would write, "If one pessimistic note ever reached my ears there were a dozen optimistic ones urging, 'Yes, you can do it. Go ahead.' As a result the thing was accomplished."

Among the classes Carver took were geology, botany, chemistry, bacteriology, zoology, and entomology (the study of insects).

Carver, like all male underclassmen, had to serve in the campus cadet battalion. And like everyone else, Carver feared General James Rush Lincoln. In Carver's opinion, General Lincoln was out to get him. It was seemingly impossible to meet Lincoln's high standards. Later, Carver came to realize Lincoln treated everyone in a similar manner. Carver eventually became amused as he observed the general's militaristic mannerisms. Hard work and a strong desire to master military science had its rewards. Carver was promoted from the rank of private to second lieutenant to first lieutenant to captain. Captain was the highest rank among the student officers. As Carver was promoted through the military ranks, his friendship with General Lincoln flourished.

Carver accepted membership in the Welch Eclectic Society, one of seven literary clubs on campus. The aim of the club was to promote "development in science, literature, and the art of public speaking." Carver viewed his mastering the art of public speaking as a special challenge. His high-pitched voice and tendency to stutter had proven embarrassing throughout his life. Once his voice unexpectedly shifted to a falsetto (artificially high voice) during his public speaking class. The teacher exclaimed, "Of all the ridiculous voices I ever heard, none has ever been quite as bad as yours!" Carver was crushed by the comment. Eventually, he forgave his teacher. The pair began to work on improving Carver's voice. Their success became evident when Carver was offered a scholarship in singing at the Boston Conservatory of Music.

By 1891, those teaching at Iowa State College of Agriculture and Mechanical Arts viewed the college as being second to none in the area of agriculture. It was the academic home of three men who were to guide the progress of agriculture in the United States for almost three decades. The three giants in agriculture were James G. Wilson, Henry Cantwell Wallace, and Henry A. Wallace.

James G. Wilson, dean of agriculture and director of the agricultural station, became the secretary of agriculture in the cabinets of three U.S. presidents—William McKinley, Theodore Roosevelt, and William Howard Taft. Henry Cantwell Wallace, assistant professor of agriculture, later became secretary of agriculture in the cabinets of President Warren G. Harding and President Calvin Coolidge. His son, Henry A. Wallace, later filled the same position during President Franklin Delano Roosevelt's first two terms. Henry A. Wallace then was elected vice president of the United States for Roosevelt's third term.

When Carver began his studies at Iowa State, the application of science to agriculture was about fifty years old. The beginnings of scientific agriculture were traceable to the work of the German chemist Baron Justus von Liebig. He had applied chemistry to plant physiology—the study of the functions and activities of plants. He taught that plants were nourished by combining carbon dioxide, nitrogen, and minerals. The atmosphere and soil were viewed as contributing to the materials used by plants. Liebig believed that fertilizers, including manure, were needed to replace minerals removed by plants. Today the ideas presented by Liebig are considered obvious. However, they were viewed as being revolutionary when Liebig first presented them.

Modern farming in England was furthered when the Agricultural Society was founded in 1838. Five years later the first agricultural experiment station was established in England.

In the United States, numerous developments were helping to make farming easier and more profitable. For example, after heavy rains in 1879 had caused a shortage of animal feeds, the process of ensilage (storing fodder in silos) became widespread. Animal vaccines and techniques for chemically analyzing soils also contributed to the expansion of farming. As new techniques were being introduced and new questions arose, Iowa State led the way in both research and teaching.

Years later Carver wrote, "Mr. [Henry C.] Wallace was one of my beloved teachers, and while his special subject in the A. & M. College was dairying in all its phases, he was a master of soils. Many are the invaluable lessons I learned from him. He set me thinking along lines practically unknown at that time...."

James G. Wilson was also influential in Carver's career. When Wilson asked Carver why he didn't seek a career along the lines of art, Carver replied, "Because I can be of more service to my race in agriculture." Wilson was impressed by Carver's humanitarian attitude.

Both Carver and Wilson were interested in religion. This interest contributed greatly to the friendship that developed between them. Iowa State students were encouraged to attend the Bible classes and prayer services sponsored by the Young Men's Christian Association (YMCA), founded in 1881. Students were also invited to attend the Sunday school classes conducted by several faculty members. Professor Wilson's Sunday school class was so popular that he was embarrassed. Privately, he requested that several students, including Carver, begin attending another class. They honored Wilson's request. However, they gradually returned.

During Carver's junior and senior years, he was Iowa State's delegate to a YMCA summer camp at Lake Geneva, Wisconsin. The daily lessons emphasized the concepts of order, precision, and promptness. Carver absorbed each lesson. Back in Ames, he pursued the Y's teachings of devotion, evangelism, education, and practicality with the zeal of a missionary.

In addition to his janitorial duties, Carver was the masseur for the Iowa State athletic teams. His duties included supervising the athletes' diets, sleep schedules, and exercise programs. He was responsible for the well-being of the track and football teams. Following workouts and athletic events, Carver would massage the players. He was noted for his ability to relieve muscle cramps, soreness, fatigue, and pulled ligaments.

At Ames, Carver maintained his practice of refusing outright charity. He would not use anything he had not paid for. It is said that when he ordered a book he would not read it until he believed the sender had received his payment.

During his first winter break of 1891–92, Carver went to Indianola and registered as a special art student in Etta Budd's class. He did the same during the second winter break of the school year. However, he became ill. When he was diagnosed as anemic—having low red blood cell production—the doctor ordered him to avoid painting for at least a year.

That winter Carver had been scheduled to go to Professor J. L. Budd's home. He was to help clean up after the Christmas Day celebration. The house was located about a mile from campus. A light snow covered the ground. Professor Budd sent a horse-drawn sleigh for Carver's ride. Dressed in old work clothes, Carver climbed into the sleigh. Carver was surprised when several students climbed in with him and the driver. As the sleigh passed through the campus, more students began to walk alongside it. Carver wondered why so many people were headed for town at the same time. In town, the sleigh was stopped in front of a big department store. Someone said, "Let's go in." Painfully aware of his clothing, Carver refused to go in. His friends dragged him into the store and over to the men's clothing section. They persuaded him to try on a suit just "to see how it would look on him." Soon he was fully dressed in a gray suit, new shoes, a hat, and gloves.

Suddenly, Professor Budd was standing before Carver. He thrust a train ticket into Carver's hands. At 7:00 P.M., Carver was on a train headed for Cedar Rapids, Iowa. Professors Budd and Wilson, along with some other friends, had used the sleigh-ride trick as a sure means of getting Carver to Cedar Rapids. An exhibition of works by Iowa artists was being held there. Carver's friends thought his works should be among those exhibited and they were.

When Carver arrived at the exhibition site, his offer to help arrange the exhibits was heartily accepted. The judges selected all four of Carver's entries to be exhibited at the World's Columbian Exposition in Chicago the following summer. This event was planned to celebrate the 400th anniversary of Christopher Columbus's trip to America. Carver decided he could only manage to take one of his four selected paintings to the World's Fair. His entry received an honorable mention.

At Iowa State, Carver used his artistic talent to produce highly detailed drawings of fungi. The fungal subjects ranged from large mushrooms to microscopic specimens, such as yeasts and mildew.

Carver also continued to perform cross-breeding experiments on plants. His favorite plants for such experiments were those producing bulbs. Carver had grown fond of bulbs during his earlier travels. It was much easier to carry bulbs than rooted plants. The college required that each student write a thesis, a presentation containing the results of original research. Carver's thesis for the bachelor's degree was *Plants as Modified by Man*. In the thesis, he described his cross-pollination experiments using the bulb-producing amaryllis, a plant with showy flowers.

Carver was elected class poet of the class of 1894. The class poem written by Carver was titled "Ode to the Gourds." Just as she had been there for Carver four years earlier, Mrs. Liston attended Carver's graduation. She was greeted by Carver at the train. He was dressed in his gray suit. In his lapel was a flower. Liston brought an armful of red carnations with her on the train. The red carnations, the class flower, were sent as special tributes from the art students at Simpson College. At the graduation dinner, Carver and Liston sat at the professors' table. Not in distance, but rather symbolically, Iowa State's first African-American graduate had come a long way—he no longer had to go to the basement to eat.

Carver would remain on campus following graduation. On October 15, 1894, Carver wrote the Milhollands: "The

Lord is wonderfully blessing me and has for these many years....And the many good things the Lord has entrusted to my care are too numerous to mention here. The last but not least I have been elected Assistant Station bottanist [botanist], I intend to take a post graduate course here, which will take two years."

During the two years spent in his position, he served as Dr. Pammel's assistant. He began to focus his attention on bacterial and fungal diseases among plants. In 1895, Carver assisted Pammel in the writing of two publications dealing with plant diseases. Working under Dr. Pammel's supervision, Carver began a mycology (fungi) collection. This collection eventually contained about twenty thousand specimens. During hikes throughout the 900-acre campus, Carver was always looking for new specimens.

One of Carver's frequent hiking partners was Henry A. Wallace, the six-year-old son of Professor Henry C. Wallace. Many years later, while serving as United States vice president, Wallace wrote:

> Because of his friendship with my father and perhaps his interest in children George Carver often took me with him on botany expeditions....Though I was a small boy he gave me credit for being able to identify different species of grasses. He made so much of it I am certain now that out of the goodness of his heart, he greatly exaggerated my botanical ability. But...his praise did me good, as praise of a child often does. There is no doubt it is the gift of the true teacher to see possibilities before the pupils themselves are conscious that they exist.

During Carver's graduate work, his friendship with James Wilson flourished. Carver was always a welcome guest at the Wilson farm in Traer, Iowa. Carver often accompanied Wilson on short lecture trips. Wilson would speak on the topic of agriculture. Carver would then address the audience with comments dealing with mycology and horticulture. He would also speak about floriculture, the cultivation and management of ornamental and flowering plants.

In November 1895, Iowa State's President William Beardshear received a letter from Westside, Mississippi. The letter was a request for Carver to join the faculty of the land-grant college of Mississippi—Alcorn Agricultural and Mechanical College. President Beardshear responded: "Mr. Carver has admirable tact and is universally liked by faculty and students....We would not care to have him change unless he can better himself...."

Carver was contacted by Alcorn officials. He was offered the chair (chairmanship) of the Agricultural Department. Carver discussed the matter with his faculty advisers.

Outstanding letters of recommendation on Carver's behalf were submitted by Dr. Pammel, Professor Budd, Professor Wilson, and General Lincoln. Wilson wrote a letter of recommendation containing several pages. Wilson wrote, in part:

> I do not want to lose Mr. Carver from our station here....
>
> We have nobody to take his place and I would never part with a student with so much regret as George Carver....It will be difficult, in fact impossible, to fill his place.
>
> ...If you should conclude to take him from us I will recognize the finger of Providence and submit.

Carver's selection as the chair, or head, of the Agricultural Department at Alcorn was for some reason postponed until the spring of 1896. In March 1896 Carver received a letter from Tuskegee, Alabama. The letter was from Booker T. Washington, the principal of Tuskegee Normal and Industrial Institute. Washington asked Carver to join his faculty. He would serve as chair of the soon-to-be-established Agricultural Department.

Booker Taliaferro Washington, like Carver, had been born into slavery. Washington's mother, Jane, and her three children had been owned by tobacco growers in Franklin County, Virginia.

Washington graduated from Hampton Normal and Agricultural Institute, Hampton, Virginia, in 1875. His principal, General Samuel C. Armstrong, would later recommend him as the individual most qualified to establish a school for blacks in Tuskegee.

On July 4, 1881, Washington founded Tuskegee Normal and Industrial School. The school, initially patterned after Hampton Institute, would undergo several name changes. Known as Tuskegee Institute for many years, Washington's school would eventually become Tuskegee University in 1985.

Washington had become an internationally known spokesperson for African Americans in September 1895. The event that made him so well known was a speech delivered in Atlanta, Georgia. The speech became widely known as the "Atlanta Compromise." Speaking before a white audience, Washington raised one arm above his head. And he exclaimed, "In all things that are purely social we [blacks and whites] can be as separate as the fingers, yet one as the hand in all things essential to mutual progress!" This was the social message his southern audience was waiting to hear. Washington had shown a willingness to accept social "compromise" between blacks and whites. It was a position later opposed by many black leaders including W. E. B. Du Bois and those who led the fight against racial segregation.

On April 3, Carver wrote to Washington: "I will finish my masters [master's] degree in scientific agr. this fall, and until then I hardly think I desire to make a change, although I expect to take up work amongst my people and have known of and appreciate the great work you are doing...." Two days later Carver advised Washington that if he were given a satisfactory position, he might leave earlier than the fall.

On April 12 Carver wrote in a lengthy letter to Washington: "[O]f course it has always been the one great ideal of my life to be of the greatest good to the greatest number of 'my people' possible and to this end I have been preparing myself for these many years; feeling as I do that this line of education is the key to unlock the golden door of freedom to our people...."

On April 17, 1896, Washington wrote Carver: "You perhaps know that at present all of our teachers are of the colored race. Now we very much prefer to have a colored man in charge of this new department and feel that you are the man for the work. If we cannot secure you we shall be forced perhaps to put in a white man.... If you are willing to come here we can pay you one thousand dollars ($1000.00) a year and board, board to include all expenses except travel.... If the terms I have named are not satisfactory we shall be willing to do anything in reason that will enable you to decide in favor of coming to Tuskegee...."

On May 16, 1896, Carver accepted Washington's offer. He closed his letter by saying, "Providence permitting I will be there in Nov."

In October 1896 Carver completed the requirements for his master of science degree in agriculture. He was so anxious to travel to Tuskegee that he decided to leave the Iowa State campus immediately. He would simply have to miss the graduation exercises in November.

Before beginning the thousand-mile train ride to Tuskegee, he was presented with a microscope as a going-away gift from his teachers and other friends at Iowa State.

George Washington Carver's Iowa State graduation picture.

8

Going Home

Carver was met at the train station in Chehaw, Alabama, by a student from Tuskegee Institute. Although the young man was late, Carver did not seem to mind. He was busily examining the plants growing along the tracks.

As the pair rode together in the surrey, Carver studied the Alabama landscape. The high banks of red and yellow clay were much more vivid than the soils of Missouri, Kansas, and Iowa. He noticed much of the surrounding land was parched and almost barren. As they continued to pass through the countryside, Carver saw vast cotton fields. African Americans of all ages were busily picking the fluffy white puffs of cotton. They placed the cotton in long sacks draped over their shoulders. The sacks extended along the ground.

Carver noticed the cabins were built of logs or rough-cut lumber. Their wooden exteriors were bleached gray by the sun and weather. Most of the yards were barren of greenery. In many yards a pig sty was located close to the cabin.

Carver noticed that the houses in Tuskegee were painted white. And the town reflected prosperity. The wagon followed the Atlanta-Montgomery highway for a mile and then turned right onto the campus. Several campus buildings were readily visible. Carver could also see the building that housed the foundry and the workshops for wheelwrights and blacksmiths. The sawmill was also noted by Carver.

Carver stepped from the surrey and began to survey the campus. He was especially eager to see the site of the future agricultural building The Armstrong-Slater Memorial Agriculture Building was to be the finest of any in the South. To Carver, the campus looked very much like a huge farm.

Carver was appointed director and instructor in scientific agriculture and dairy science. He was provided with assistants in the areas of farm management, stock raising, truck gardening, horticulture, and dairying. He began his work in October 1896. He had thirteen students and no well-defined course of study. By the end of the school year in May 1897, he had made considerable progress. He had enrolled twenty-six students, including three women. He also had developed a two-year curriculum patterned after his classes at Iowa State.

Carver designed the interior layout for the new agricultural building. The first floor housed classrooms. A lecture room, a reading room, and a herbarium—a collection of dried plant specimens arranged for study—were located on the second floor. The basement was used to house the dairy equipment.

Carver's department was constantly being given added responsibilities. For example, Carver worked closely with the chief of the weather bureau in Montgomery, the state capital. This activity kept him busy measuring rainfall, displaying weather flags, and sending daily weather reports. As chair of the Sanitary Committee, he was responsible for testing the safety of the drinking water throughout Macon County.

Carver had to equip his laboratory. The school was short of funds. Carver knew he would have to make his equipment. He would tell the students, "There is no need to whine, 'Oh, if I only had so and so!'" He would tell them, "Do it anyhow; use what you find about you." He would then accompany the students to the trash piles. The students would search through the trash for usable items such as bottles, jars, wire, rubber, pieces of glass, and string. A horseshoe became the classroom bell. Carver found an oil lamp. He used it not only to warm his hands, but also to heat chemicals, and as a light source for his microscope. Since chemicals were expensive, Carver would use readily available sources. Discarded fruit-jar lids became his source of zinc.

Carver's habits of thrift were legendary. He was always able to save money. One preserved note reads: "Professor Carver, please let me have seventy-five dollars to be returned at earliest convenience. Booker Washington."

Carver was ahead of his time in many respects. The scavenger hunts with his students were an early example of the conservation of natural resources. He was teaching the recycling of natural resources, by example, several decades before the practice was promoted by large numbers of ecological experts.

Carver taught that simply saving something without a sense of order was a waste of time and effort. To illustrate his point, he would show the students a box of assorted strings, saved, but thoroughly tangled. "That is ignorance," he would say. He would then display a box in which the salvaged strings were either neatly tied or rolled into balls, adding, "And this is intelligence."

Until Carver's arrival at Tuskegee, farming was an unpopular topic among the students. Some of the teachers would even assign farm tasks as a form of punishment for misbehavior. The students viewed farming as being neither a meaningful trade nor a professional career.

Working under Carver, students found farming both enjoyable and practical. Carver possessed two essential characteristics of a good teacher—a thorough knowledge of the subject and insight into how to get the students to learn.

Carver was impatient with students who lacked personal motivation. He would say, "I will help you as long as you are making progress, but once you decide to quit, I will not waste my own time further. And don't take up any of my time with a frivolous excuse. All I want is the thing done."

He was also intolerant of the word "About." He would say, "There are only two ways: one is right and the other is wrong. About is always wrong. Don't tell me it's about right. If it's only about right, then it's wrong."

Among the students it was widely believed that Carver could identify any plant. However, there was the possibility that he might be fooled with respect to the animal kingdom. At least that is what some of the students in one of his entomology classes thought. One day they brought in an insect pinned to a piece of cardboard. One student excitedly said, "We just found this strange bug, Professor. What is it?" Carver began to examine the strange specimen. It had the head of a large ant, the body of a beetle, the legs of a spider, the antennae of a moth, all carefully glued together. Finally, Carver announced with an air of seriousness, "Well, this, I think, is what we call a humbug." Everyone laughed, includ-

This photograph of some of the faculty at Tuskegee was taken in about 1898. Carver is the man standing on the far left in the third row.

ing Carver. He was delighted by such displays of imagination and creativity.

Carver considered every place a potential classroom. People could be taught in a garden, a cornfield, a cotton patch, or a formal classroom. Wherever Carver met a farmer, he believed he could help him. Carver had journeyed to Tuskegee with the aim of helping the southern farmers. The Experiment Station at Tuskegee Institute became one of the main ways of dispensing helpful agricultural information among the farmers, especially those who were African Americans.

Although the results of the experiments were to be published in bulletins, these booklets were useless to individuals who could not read. Farmers were urged to send samples of soils, fertilizers, insects, water, and diseased plants to the station. They were also invited to visit the station throughout the year.

The Experiment Station consisted of twenty acres of land near the agricultural building. The land was divided into plots and various crops were planted. Carver supervised. The students did the cultivating. Detailed records were kept as each plot and crop was prepared. The records included an analysis of the soil, the amount of specific fertilizer added, the type of crop planted, and the history of the crop from planting through harvesting. The recording of the observations was essential. This was the reason for conducting the experiments. The results of the most successful experiments could be passed on to the farmers. Even the results of crop failures were useful. They indicated which growing conditions were to be avoided.

Carver came to realize poor farmers could not afford commercial fertilizer. Nor did they own the livestock needed to provide enough manure. However, they did have enough organic waste available to improve their crops. He gained this insight while rummaging through a trash heap. He noticed a thriving pumpkin vine growing among the trash. The vine had several runners loaded with pumpkins.

Carver began a compost pile. A wooden pen was constructed. The pen was piled with organic (plant and animals) waste as well as paper, discarded clothing, leaves, rags, grass, and weeds. Rich soil brought from the nearby woods and swamps was used to cover the heap. As the material decayed, it was applied as fertilizer to the station soil.

Carver also began to enrich the soil by planting legumes, pod-producing plants. This group of seed plants includes beans, peas, clover, vetch, and peanuts. These plants are unique. Whenever specific bacteria living in the soil invade the roots of legumes, small swellings form along the roots. The tiny swellings are called nodules. The bacteria

This photo shows a much older Carver carrying a specimen box in which he collected plant samples.

65

living in the nodules are called nitrogen-fixing bacteria. This is because they "fix," or combine, atmospheric nitrogen with other elements to form compounds called nitrates and nitrites. As the legumes die, the nitrogen compounds are added to the soil as fertilizer. The atmosphere, including air between soil particles, contains 78 percent nitrogen. Thus, nitrogen is readily available to the legumes.

In 1896, Carver planted crimson (red) clover, cowpea, and hairy vetch. A year later he planted velvet beans and began experimenting with the peanut, *Arachis hypogaea*, which was not considered a farm crop. Carver also began planting the soja pea. Today, we know the soja pea as the soybean, *Glycine max*.

Carver and Washington knew that cotton, planted year after year for decades, had removed the nutrients from the soil throughout much of the South. The mineral-poor soil was unable to provide lush crops. In the South, at that time, the one popular crop remained "King" Cotton. The two men knew it would take years to convince the farmers to abandon cotton as their major crop. Thus, they would try to improve cotton production.

Carver decided to produce some improved varieties of cotton, *Gossypium*. He would do so through cross-fertilization. By 1909, he would develop four new varieties, all adapted to the sandy soils of Macon County. Seeds and the directions for cross-fertilizing specific varieties of cotton were mailed to any farmer who requested them. At the time Carver first went to Tuskegee some of the cotton varieties were producing two bolls per stalk. In comparison, some of the improved varieties yielded as many as 275 bolls per stalk without the use of commercial fertilizer. The local farmers were amazed that Carver, who had never grown cotton before, could grow better cotton than they could.

Carver had an open-door policy at the Experiment Station. He was never too busy to answer someone's questions. However, he decided that he would be more successful by giving information before larger groups. To bring groups of farm couples to the station, Carver began the Farmers' Institute in the fall of 1897. Thereafter, the event was scheduled for the third Tuesday of each month. The monthly event attracted about seventy-five persons. Most of them lived within twenty-five miles of the campus. Speaking in simple terms, Carver would discuss crop rotation, dairying, raising poultry, and the prevention of erosion. The group would visit plots where they were shown heads of cabbage weighing twenty pounds and onions seven inches in diameter.

In 1898, it was decided to hold a fair so the farmers could display their best produce, canned goods, and handicrafts. Every year after that the fair increased in size and popularity. By 1903, the institute was invited to participate in the state fair held in Montgomery. Carver had his own exhibition booth at the state fair. He displayed dried foods and soybeans and demonstrated the value of the sweet potato and cowpeas.

February became an exciting time at Tuskegee. The Farmers' Institute and the Farmers' Annual Conference, which was begun by Washington in 1890, were scheduled to meet at the same time. On the eve of the joint meeting, hundreds of people would begin arriving on campus. The night air would be filled with the smell of hickory smoke and barbecue. Student chefs would spend the night turning and basting the meat. Farmers spent the evening decorating their wagons for the next day's parade. The parade and crowd of spectators would end at the campus chapel.

Washington would stand on a platform and welcome the

guests. He would encourage them to continue with their farming. Individual farmers would be invited to give testimony concerning their success. At noon dinner was served.

During the afternoon, the guests toured the campus buildings and the Experiment Station. Carver provided a demonstration booth and was kept busy all day. For example, at that time many people thought tomatoes were poisonous. He would cook tomatoes and eat some to prove they were not at all poisonous. He would then offer some of the tomatoes to those standing around the booth. He would demonstrate eighteen ways to prepare cowpeas for the table. He would encourage the wives to imagine each meal as being a work of art. Each deserved as much attention as a fine painting.

The merrymaking would continue for several hours after sunset. The visitors would then begin their journey home. Some left in wagons, others on the backs of mules. Many had to walk.

In 1903, the male students at the institute moved into a newly constructed dormitory, Rockefeller Hall. The new dormitory also became the residence of Professor Carver. He moved into some rooms on the first floor. Those rooms became Carver's residence for almost forty years. His collections of books, paintings, rocks, plants, and handicrafts were displayed throughout his rooms.

One day while Carver was about thirty miles from Tuskegee he made a discovery that was "out of this world." He stumbled upon a meteorite, which he hauled to his residence. It is probable that this meteorite had fallen to the ground many years earlier. The night of Tuesday, November 12, 1833, had become the legendary "Night the Stars Fell on Alabama." Many of the elderly citizens of the South used that evening as a historical reference point. They would say that some event had occurred either before or after "the stars fell." The sky was clear the night of November 12. But at about 11 P.M., the sky began to fill with shooting stars (meteors). By 3 A.M., thousands of people were standing outdoors, most in their nightclothes, watching the sky. The heavenly display was reported to have been spectacular. While the shower of stars is connected to Alabama history, both in books and song, it was seen throughout the South. Carver added the meteorite to the collection of items in his rooms.

Carver was restless. He maintained a lifelong ritual of rising at four o'clock each morning. He then would go into the woods. He would say, "Alone there with the things I love most, I gather my specimens and study the lessons Nature is so eager to teach us all. Nothing is more beautiful than the loneliness of the woods before sunrise. At no other time have I so sharp an understanding of what God means to do with me as in those early hours of dawn. When other folks are still asleep, I hear God best and learn His plan." One of Carver's colleagues noted, "The first thing each morning, George asks God's will, and then spends the rest of the day doing it."

Carver was always extracting—removing by physical or chemical means—materials from both the soil and plants. He would also mix the extracted materials with the hope of discovering some useful products. Carver's fascination with the clays of Alabama continued from the day he arrived at the train station in Chehaw. He extracted whitewash from white clay. He extracted a water-soluble bluing from rotten sweet potatoes. By adding the blue pigment extracted from the sweet potatoes to yellow clay, he produced a green color washing, or dye. Once Carver had made these early discoveries, his imagination began to explode with enthusiasm. He eventually produced at least twenty-seven color washings by combining various color extractions.

Using clay, Carver painted landscapes and still lifes. On occasion, individuals would ask him how long he expected the colors in his paintings to last. He would direct their attention to the exposed hillsides. He would remind the individuals that the pigments in the clay had remained vivid for thousands of years. Surely, the pigments would survive for a long time on canvas.

In 1902 Carver made an outstanding discovery. Near Montgomery he noticed a brilliant red bank of clay. He collected a pail of the clay and took it back to his laboratory. Carver detected blue pigment in the clay. After a series of chemical experiments, Carver produced a beautiful blue pigment from the clay. The pigment could be mixed with either water or oil. The discovery was proudly exhibited by Carver at fairs. News about this pigment reached paint manufacturers. One large paint manufacturer sent a technician to Tuskegee.

Carver explained that the ancient Egyptians were especially fond of this long-lost blue pigment. They used it to paint the interior of their tombs so they could sleep with it for eternity. The technician remarked to Carver, "According to our observation this is seventy times bluer than blue." He informed Carver that his company would like to put the pigment on the market. "No, no, no!, Carver exclaimed. "I don't want to commercialize it." Later, however, Carver was persuaded to obtain a patent to protect his discovery. To obtain a patent means to register an idea and design with the government. A patent is a government document giving the inventor rights to the invention for a limited time. A patent gives the inventor the right to prevent others from making, using, or selling the invention. Despite Carver's patent, within a year the paint company announced the discovery of

Carver carried on research dealing with pigments and clay. This photograph shows him in his laboratory at Tuskegee Institute.

a "new and improved" blue. Carver did not sue. He had neither the money nor the time to challenge the company in court.

Carver believed that his findings were provided freely by the Creator. Since they had not cost him anything, he didn't believe it was morally right for him to charge for their use. Carver seldom applied for a patent. He knew the securing of patents would attract hordes of people who wished to benefit financially. Carver knew that if he became involved with the idea of making large sums of money he would neglect his research. When Carver would display a new product, someone would invariably ask, "Now, what are you going to do with it?" Carver would reply, "I've done all I intend to. My interest is scientific and not financial. If an investigator goes into business, he ceases to be an investigator—that is the business of the businessman."

Carver's mail often contained requests for advice. Many times the letters would contain checks. The senders wanted to show their appreciation for Carver's time and effort. Sometimes a company would send a check in appreciation for some benefit gained through Carver's research. The checks would be returned to the senders. Carver did not charge for his services.

One of Carver's favorite means of spreading information among farmers was the publication of a series of bulletins. These bulletins were booklets containing information which had been organized by Carver. Much of the information was not original. Carver used the bulletins to dispense both new and old information that he thought would benefit the farmers. He wrote the bulletins in easy-to-understand wording. Carver's first bulletin, *Feeding Acorns to Livestock*, was issued in 1898. It was followed later the same year by *Experiments with Sweet Potatoes*. In 1899, Carver issued

Fertilizer Experiments with Cotton. By 1913 Carver had written and distributed twenty-five bulletins.

These bulletins were only one of many ways Carver tried to reach the farmers who could not visit the campus. He realized that many of the sharecroppers lacked adequate transportation. Carver concluded that if the farmers could not come to him, he would go to them. On Friday evenings, he would fill a mule-drawn wagon with an assortment of supplies. Sometimes accompanied by another teacher, he would travel throughout the countryside. As Carver made his way down the rural roads, he would pull his wagon into countless yards. He would introduce himself and say he was from the institute. He would then offer his services and advice.

Carver, the teacher, made the farmers' yards and fields his classroom. He would later return to see if his lessons were heeded. Carver made many friends for himself and the institute through these rural excursions.

Carver also enjoyed visiting the townsfolk in Tuskegee. He always carried some item that would catch the attention of passersby. He enjoyed discussing the item with both black and white citizens.

Carver enjoyed his weekend trips. Yet, the need was too great to be met by so few trips. Agriculturists in Europe had experimented with the idea of movable schools. In 1904, Iowa State proved itself again to be in the forefront of agricultural education. In that year, Iowa State began the operation of movable schools in the United States with "Seed Corn Gospel Trains." These trains carried lecturers and demonstration materials to railroad stations to meet crowds of awaiting farmers.

Washington suggested to Carver that a properly equipped wagon might be suitable as a full-time "traveling agricultural school." The wagon would visit farms on a regular basis and be operated by a full-time instructor. Carver liked the idea and submitted a proposal for the project. His proposal included a sketch of a wagon that could carry an assortment of equipment, including dairy equipment. The wagon would also be equipped with large charts showing the various aspects of farming. Carver also suggested some topics to be covered by lecturers.

Washington secured the money to equip and operate the wagon from Morris K. Jesup, a New York banker and philanthropist, and the John F. Slater Fund. The wagon was made by the students at Tuskegee. It was named the "Jesup Agricultural Wagon." Tuskegee's movable school began its operation on May 24, 1906. George R. Bridgeforth was appointed full-time operator of the Jesup Wagon.

Bridgeforth often obtained the permission of farmers to use their land as demonstration sites. Seaman A. Knapp, a special agent for the United States Department of Agriculture (USDA), liked this aspect of the Jesup Wagon project. Knapp visited Tuskegee in 1906. He had been hired by the USDA as special agent in charge of the Farmers' Cooperative Demonstration Work with the assigned duty of establishing farm demonstration programs. He had earlier proven his own success in such a program dealing with eliminating the boll weevil in Texas. Weevils are a type of beetle having a long snout. The boll weevil eats the developing pod of cotton (the boll).

Washington noted Knapp's interest in the Jesup Wagon. He suggested that the Jesup Wagon be made a part of the USDA program. Knapp agreed with Washington's suggestion. In 1906 Thomas M. Campbell, one of Carver's outstanding students, was appointed as the first African-American demonstration agent. When he made his first

George Washington Carver enjoyed working in his laboratory.

visits to several schools in western Alabama, Professor Carver went along for encouragement. Later, another Tuskegee graduate, John B. Pierce, was appointed as the second African-American demonstration agent. Together, Campbell and Pierce were very effective in spreading Carver's ideas throughout the South.

The Jesup Agricultural Wagon was later replaced by a truck. The Movable School then became known as the Booker T. Washington School on Wheels. Its services were extended throughout the state of Alabama.

During the summer of 1908 Carver traveled to Neosho and Diamond Grove. In Neosho, he visited Aunt Mariah Watkins and inspected the Lincoln School. In Diamond Grove he greeted Uncle Mose. Moses was quite frail. He was now a widower almost 100 years old. As a parting gift, George was given his mother's spinning wheel. Uncle Mose died in 1910.

9

Campus Life

Carver was a man of contrasts. Among his co-workers, he was known as a loner. He rarely attended social affairs. He enjoyed solitude, and he was also a victim of shyness.

Whenever someone ventured to ask Carver why he had never married, he had several ready answers such as, "Now what woman would want a husband trailing soil specimens around her parlor? And how could I explain to a wife that I have to go outdoors at four o'clock every morning to talk to flowers."

Carver seriously considered marriage in 1905. Carver, was reluctant to talk about the affair. He simply said he and the woman realized they did not share the same goals.

Although Carver rarely socialized with his colleagues, the opposite was true with respect to his students. He enjoyed time spent with young people. He offered them advice and reminded them to use good manners. A simple

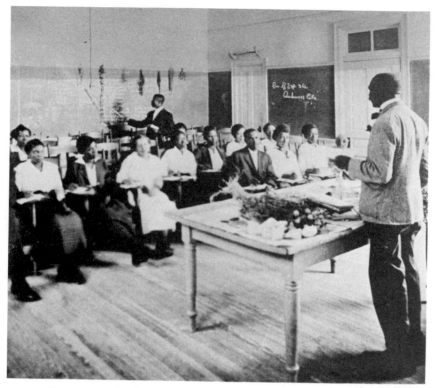

Carver taught classes at the Tuskegee Institute for many years.

inquiry such as, "Has the tipping of hats to ladies gone out of fashion?" would cause them to be more thoughtful the next time.

Carver helped many students financially. He aided any student, male or female, if he could. And he tried to help them secretly without causing embarrassment.

Sunday became the favorite day for student visits with Carver. On that day, the teacher could spend uninterrupted time conversing with the visitors. The nature of the Sabbath also tended to direct Carver's thoughts and comments to reflect upon the Scriptures and their relevance to life and nature. Many students enjoyed Carver's comments regarding the Bible. They eventually persuaded him to begin a Bible class. The class was scheduled between dinner and chapel services. The reading of Scripture would begin at 6 o'clock. The Bible class was initially held in Rockefeller Hall, but was moved about as the audience increased. By 1911 the class had about one hundred regular attendees. When the number of people attending reached about three hundred, the meetings were held in the Carnegie Library.

Carver's personal time was rather limited. Yet he spent much of it writing. In addition to the bulletins, Carver wrote numerous research papers. He also wrote a newspaper column, "Professor Carver's Advice." Several magazine articles were written by Carver. His personal correspondence also took up large amounts of time.

Nevertheless, Carver found time to isolate and study fungi. Years later numerous articles appearing in scientific journals would remind the readers of Carver's contributions to the field of mycology. Several fungal species were named to honor Carver, including *Taphrina carveri, Colletotrichum carveri*, and *Metasphaeria carveri*. Carver was so protective of his specimens, including his fungal collection, that no one else was permitted to clean his rooms.

Carver was not one to follow the latest fashion trends. He often wore old, improperly fitted clothing. His suits were often secondhand ones. Yet each morning he picked a flower and placed it in his lapel as he walked to his laboratory.

Whenever anyone made a remark regarding his clothing, Carver had a witty rebuttal. When someone asked, "Professor, why in the world did you have your picture taken with that checkered collar?" Carver responded, "I had it on."

Carver's early years at Tuskegee were plagued by frustration. He was upset over a lack of funds. He felt that he was being overburdened. Yet, he was offended by attempts to take certain responsibilities away from him. He was offended whenever Washington reprimanded him for certain failures.

When Carver began working at Tuskegee, he was given special treatment. He expected it thereafter. His starting salary was at least twice that of the other instructors. When he arrived on campus, he requested two rooms in which to live. At that time, each bachelor teacher was expected to share a single room with another teacher. When Carver failed to obtain satisfactory living quarters, he wrote to the members of the institute's finance committee.

During the following two years Carver became increasingly frustrated. On May 30, 1898, he wrote to Booker T. Washington complaining about being overworked. He also resented having to work with incompetent people and not having adequate supplies.

Dear Sir:—

I assure you that no one is more deeply interested in the welfare of the school than myself, and especially my Dept. I have labored early and late and at times beyond my physical strength....

Here I am working with the smallest and most inexperienced staff of any station in the U.S....It is impossible for me to do this work without men and means....If I thought things were to run as they have always run I would not stay here any longer than I could get away....

Carver thought the situation at Tuskegee in 1898 was bad. The worst was yet to come. He and George R. Bridgeforth had not met. In 1902 their fateful meeting occurred. Carver soon regretted his decision to approve the hiring of Bridgeforth. As soon as Bridgeforth joined the faculty he decided he could do a better job than Carver.

Carver was quiet and secretive; Bridgeforth was brash and outspoken. Bridgeforth was not reluctant to criticize Carver. He sent letters to both Carver and Washington criticizing Carver's ability to manage his department. Even Washington was painfully aware of Carver's inability to operate the campus poultry yard.

In 1904 Carver was reprimanded by Washington for his possible involvement in falsifying unfavorable poultry reports. Carver was humiliated. He also offered to resign. Washington ignored the offer.

Bridgeforth saw this conflict between the principal and Carver as a chance to further his career. He encouraged Washington to relieve Carver of some responsibilities. Washington formed a committee to evaluate Bridgeforth's recommendations. The committee recommended dividing the responsibilities in the Agriculture Department between Carver and Bridgeforth. Carver would be named the director of Agricultural Instruction and Experiment Station. Bridgeforth would become the director of Agricultural Industries. The operations within the department would be divided along the lines of the theoretical (research) and the applied (practical).

Carver rejected the proposal. He informed Washington that his new title was "too far a drop downward." He added, "A few at Tuskegee will understand it but the public never." He also submitted his resignation, "[T]he above and much more...causes me to ask that you kindly accept my resignation....I shall...turn the books over in good shape so the work need not suffer....

On November 14, 1904, Carver penned another letter to Washington. Carver had reviewed the situation and was more understanding. Carver retained both his title and control of the poultry yard.

By 1908, however, the petty bickering between Carver and Bridgeforth made some changes necessary. The recommendations submitted four years earlier were accepted. The Agriculture Department was divided. Carver and Bridgeforth were given the titles and responsibilities as outlined in the earlier report.

In 1910 Washington reassigned some of Carver's responsibilities. Carver was named director of the Department of Research and Experiment Station. Carver was not pleased. And his feuding with Bridgeforth continued. On May 14, 1912, Carver submitted a list of broken promises made by the principal. Carver reminded Washington that for "16 years I have worked without a single dollar's increase in salary...." After listing the unfulfilled promises, Carver added, "All of the above facts and others, together with your note of May 3d. to the effect that my teaching was unsatisfactory, places me in a very embarrassing position. I interpret the above to mean that the school is real[l]y tired of my services and wishes me to resign. I see no alternative, Am I correct[?]."

This offer to resign was ignored by Washington, as were most of the others. However, by 1913 Washington apparently was growing intolerant of Carver's continuous habit of threatening to resign. Washington wrote, "I would suggest, also, in connection with this whole matter that before next March you decide definitely what you want to do: If you want to stay in the service of the school I should be glad to have you, if not, I think you should decide to withdraw. You cannot do justice to yourself or to the school when you are in an unsettled state of mind. The proposition of your going or remaining has come up, as you know, a good many times in the past few years, and I think it is best for all concerned for the matter to be decided definitely by next March."

From the foregoing one might mistakenly conclude that the relationship between Carver and Washington was solely marked by discord and bitterness. Such was not the case. Washington was quick to praise Carver in those areas in which Carver excelled. In 1911, the principal wrote Carver, "You are a great teacher, a great lecturer, a great inspirer of young men and old men; that is your fort[e] [strength] and we have all been trying as best we could to help you do the work for which you are best fitted and to leave aside that for which you are least fitted." Washington also noted, "You have great ability in original research, in making experiments in the soil and elsewhere on untried plants. You have great ability in the direction of showing what can be done in the use of foods and the preserving of foods."

Carver and Washington held each other in high esteem. Their relationship was cemented by bonds of mutual respect and admiration. The impish Carver was caught by the principal on at least one occasion stealing some onions from his private garden. While the two laughed at the seemingly awkward situation, Carver handed the principal some edible weeds that he had gathered for him.

Sometimes Carver would be roused from his sleep by a knock on his door. The young man serving as night guard would begin to explain to Carver the reason for disturbing him. "Mr. Washington would like to know if you..." Without needing to hear further, Carver would respond, "Of course. Tell Mr. Washington I'll be right out." The two men would walk around the darkened campus. Washington's heavy burdens would seem to become lighter as they talked. Washington knew he could always find greater peace of mind in the company of Carver. Eventually, the two friends would stroll back to Rockefeller Hall. The guard would hear them say, "Good night, Professor." "Good night, Mr. Washington."

Occasionally, someone would speak to Carver regarding Washington's habit of disrupting his sleep. The professor, however, always defended Washington's actions. He would say, "Whenever Mr. Washington calls, I shall be ready. I consider it an honor and a privilege."

In early November 1915 Washington was hospitalized during a visit to New York. Realizing he was near death the principal decided to return to his beloved campus. Dr. Booker T. Washington died November 14, 1915, only hours after reaching his campus residence "The Oaks." He was buried in the campus cemetery located near the chapel.

Isaac Fisher, president of the Tuskegee Alumni Association, voiced the sentiments of many as he said, "With the death of Dr. Washington, closes one chapter of Negro history. The whole world is poorer today because he has gone."

10

The Work Continues

The death of Booker T. Washington was a great personal loss for Carver. During the months immediately following Washington's death, Carver was deeply depressed. His grief was evident to everyone. He was too upset even to attempt teaching. In order to provide Carver some sense of being useful, he was given the duty of supervising the activities during "study hour."

Carver only began to recover when he became actively involved in fund-raising. The money was to be used to build the Booker T. Washington Memorial on campus. Carver donated six months' salary to the memorial fund. In a letter to Emmett Jay Scott, Washington's secretary, Carver wrote, "I am sure Mr. Washington never knew how much I loved him, and the cause for which he gave his life."

The passing of Washington saddened those associated with Tuskegee. However, someone had to carry his work forward. The role of school principal was assumed by Major Robert Russa Moton. The new principal, like his predecessor, was brought in from Hampton Institute.

Unlike Washington, however, Moton enjoyed a completely warm and cordial relationship with Carver. The new principal respected Carver and his contributions to Tuskegee. He viewed Carver as a trusted partner rather than as a subordinate, that is, someone holding a lower position. Moton was very supportive of Carver. Whereas, Washington was likely to answer Carver's complaints with demands, Moton tried to make Carver happy. Moton used both tact and flattery in dealing with Carver. Shortly after Washington's death, Carver notified the Academic Department that he would be unable to teach botany in the fall. In response to Carver's notice, Moton wrote: "I wish you would withhold your definite decision until I have a chance to talk with you....I need not tell you that it will be impossible to get anybody to teach this subject as you have done, and I do not like to think of the students losing the inspiration and help that would come by your teaching." In the fall, Carver taught his botany classes.

A year later when Carver tried to give up his teaching assignments, Moton's comments to Carver were even more flattering. Moton wrote, " I hope it may be possible for you this year to take at least one period, selecting any subject that seems to you advisable. I know how taxed [overburdened] you are, and I hesitate to add anything to your already very heavy program, but I am anxious to have as many students as possible come in direct contact with you. I know of no other persons who can give the inspiration, saying nothing about the technical instruction that you can give."

Carver's status as a member of the Executive Council also received a boost under Moton's leadership. In 1916 the minutes of the Executive Council began to include praise for Carver and his accomplishments. Carver became the only council member to be addressed with the title "Professor" rather than "Mister." In the fall of that year, Carver received two outstanding honors. First he was invited to join the Advisory Board of the National Agricultural Society. Second, he was elected a Fellow, that is, member, of England's Royal Society for the Encouragement of Arts, Manufacturers and Commerce. The election of an African American to this prestigious organization, which was founded in 1754, was recognized as a tremendous honor. The news media coverage of this event made Carver an internationally recognized figure. By association with Carver, Tuskegee Institute also received the benefits of widespread publicity.

Carver was able to gradually reduce the amount of time he spent teaching. He also lost most of his interest in the Experiment Station. In 1916 only two projects were conducted at the station.

As Carver spent more time in his laboratory, his publishing of bulletins also declined. In 1916 he published two bulletins containing information from earlier work. One of the bulletins was *How to Grow the Peanut and 105 Ways of Preparing It for Human Consumption.* The other bulletin was *Three Delicious Meals Every Day for the Farmer.* This bulletin provided several recipes that required very few purchased items.

In December 1916 Carver gave Emmett J. Scott a list of products that, according to Carver, were "now ready for the [commercial] market." After reviewing the list Scott saw a potential market for a rubber substitute derived from the sweet potato. Carver, however, believed the product needed to be studied further. Carver stated that his wood stains were the products that were the "cheapest, easiest and best to go into with small capital [money]." Carver also highly recommended the marketing of his calcimines (white or tinted liquid used to coat plastered walls), toilet powders, cleansing agents, and feather products. However, the marketing of these products did not take place. The same fate awaited another commercial product. In February 1917 Carver announced that a local company would market a mixed food for cattle. Carver had provided the research in determining this nutritious mixture.

As early as 1917 Carver began to spend as much time away from Tuskegee as he did on campus. In February 1917, for example, he attended farmers' conferences in four states. As he visited various colleges to give lectures, his return visits were added to his calendar. In 1917 Carver named clays, sands, and the crops suitable for growth in Alabama as his three major lines of research. During the same year he issued three bulletins: *Twelve Ways to Meet the New Economic Conditions Here in the South, Forty-three Ways to Save the Wild Plum Crop,* and *How to Grow the Cow Pea and 40 Ways to Prepare It as a Table Delicacy.*

Carver's expanded laboratory research and extensive lecturing tours enabled him to limit his teaching load. His classwork became limited to his teaching during the summer sessions. For six to ten weeks each summer he taught schoolteachers from all over the South. They traveled to Tuskegee for refresher courses and advanced study. Carver would maintain this activity until the 1930s when his health began to get much worse.

Even though Carver was no longer actively teaching during the regular school year, he still found time to associate with the students. His Sunday evening Bible class remained popular. By the end of 1920 the number of students enrolled in the Bible class would exceed two hundred.

For some of the Tuskegee students Carver became a substitute father. They continued to write to him for many years after they graduated. Some of the letters asked Carver for advice in dealing with racial prejudice in society. The students had been sheltered from racial bigotry while enrolled at Tuskegee. However, they quickly ran into it beyond the campus, including the military.

In 1918 Carver issued three bulletins: *How to Grow the Tomato and 105 Ways to Prepare It as Table Delicacy*, *How to Make Sweet Potato Flour, Starch, Bread, Sugar and Mock Cocoanut*, and *How the Farmer Can Save His Sweet Potatoes*. Carver would not publish another bulletin for nine years. The lack of newly released bulletins was merely a reflection of Carver's busy schedule in other areas, including the increased production and utilization of food.

With the entry of the United States into World War I in April 1917, the government became concerned with food production.

In January 1918 officials in the United States Department of Agriculture invited Carver to visit them in Washington, D.C. They were interested in Carver's use of the sweet potato in making flour. Plans were developed for the construction of a machine that could dry 10,0000 bushels of sweet potatoes and convert the dried material to flour. Although the flour-making device was not installed in Tuskegee, much to Carver's disappointment, Carver was consulted throughout the project. The end of the war in late 1918 ended the nation's wheat shortage. The government stopped its flour-producing experiment.

During the same year Thomas Edison expressed an

Carver at work. He developed hundreds of products from plants such as peanuts and sweet potatoes and tried to make southern farmers less dependent upon cotton as their main crop.

interest in hiring Carver as a research partner. A representative of Edison was sent to interview Carver and make a salary offer. Carver was always vague in his later discussions of the salary offer. Some sources place the salary figure as high as $200,000 which would have been an extremely generous offer at the time. Years later, Carver would say he declined the offer because of the greater agricultural possibilities in the South as well as the greater need for his services in the South.

In 1919 Carver's work with the peanut gained national attention. During that year, he developed a process for making "peanut milk." On September 22, 1919, Carver notified Dr. Moton of his discovery. He wrote to Moton, "I am sure you will be pleased to know that I have today made a delicious and wholesome milk from peanuts." About a week later the news about the new milk-producing process had reached Walter M. Grubbs. Grubbs was associated with the Peanut Products Corporation in Birmingham, Alabama. He wrote Carver concerning the new process. Carver assured Grubbs that the peanut milk tasted as good as cow's milk and had been shown to be suitable for cooking and cheese production. Grubbs was so enthusiastic about Carver's claim of "unlimited possibilities" regarding the process that he went to Tuskegee to see for himself.

Grubbs was impressed by Carver and his products. He urged Carver to speak at the upcoming dedication of a monument in Coffee County. The citizens of Enterprise, Alabama, had erected a monument honoring the cotton-devouring boll weevil. The people were showing their appreciation to the insect for its unsuspected role in curing the South of its dependency on cotton. They were now planting other crops including the peanut. The invitation to speak in Enterprise signaled the beginning of Carver's relationship with the peanut industry.

Carver was invited to address the delegates attending a convention of the United Peanut Growers' Association of America. The convention was to be held in Montgomery at the Exchange Hotel. It was from this building that the Confederate Congress had sent the telegram authorizing the military attack on Fort Sumter thus beginning the Civil War. The convention began on Monday, September 13, 1920. The weather was almost unbearably hot.

On Tuesday morning Carver arrived in Montgomery. In his satchels he had packed some twenty-five or thirty bottles containing peanut products. Carrying his heavy load, Carver presented himself to the hotel doorman. The doorman told him that the convention of peanut growers was being held at City Hall. When he arrived at City Hall he was told that the group had been there but had left. When Carver arrived back at the hotel he was forbidden to enter. African Americans were not allowed inside. The doorman finally agreed to have a note written by Carver delivered to the group. A bellhop was summoned to deliver the note. When it was agreed that Carver could enter the hotel, he had to use the rear entrance. Carver then had to use a freight elevator to reach the meeting room.

Although tired and perspiring, Carver gave no hint of the trouble he had endured. As he addressed the assembled delegates, he began to remove the bottles from his satchels. As he removed each bottle, he identified its contents. His display included leather stains ranging in color from black to tan to reddish brown; wood stains, including peacock blue and malachite green; Worcestershire sauce; buttermilk; cream; evaporated milk; fruit punch; ground coffee; instant coffee; and instant coffee with cream. All of the products were made from the peanut. At the conclusion of his talk, Carver received loud applause and was offered help in securing patents for his products.

After Carver spoke, Congressman H. B. Steagall praised Carver for his work. He noted that Carver's discoveries were testimony to the tremendous potential of the peanut as the raw material for industrial products. He proposed that the association lobby Congress for a tariff on imported peanuts. Such a tax would make foreign-grown peanuts more expensive and so would protect the interests of

American farmers. He added, "When the time comes that this question must be thrashed out before the American Congress I propose to see that Professor Carver is there in order that he may instruct them a little about peanuts, as he has done here on this occasion." Steagall's comments were heartily endorsed by loud applause.

In January 1921 Carver received a telegram from the United Peanut Growers' Association officials: "Want you in Washington...depending on you to show Ways and Means Committee Possibilities of the peanut." Carver replied that he would attend the hearings regarding the General Tariff Revision. The hearings would be made before the U.S. House of Representatives' Ways and Means Committee.

A few days later, Carver sat throughout a long day of hearings—committee meetings in which witnesses presented evidence and information. He was horrified by the hearings. He was shocked by the arguments and conduct of the participants. He was unprepared for the rudeness. Some members of Congress seemed to imply that witnesses were liars. He was intimidated by the lengthy briefs (written summaries of testimony) that had been submitted to the committee weeks earlier. No one had mentioned to him that the submitting of a brief was expected.

Carver's name was called at four o'clock. As he made his way forward, one congressman said, "I suppose if you have plenty of peanuts and watermelons you're perfectly happy?" Carver ignored the remark. The committee chairperson said, "All right, Mr. Carver. We will give you 10 minutes." After explaining that he had been invited to speak on behalf of the United Peanut Growers' Association, Carver began to display his assorted products. In a humorous remark addressing Prohibition (the laws against the making, transporting, or selling of alcoholic drinks), the chairperson said, "If you have anything to drink, don't put it under the table." Carver quickly responded, "I am not ready to use them just now. They will come later if my 10 minutes are extended." The hearing room filled with laughter. Another congressman said, "Let us have order. This man knows a great deal about this business." As Carver continued, he said, "Here is a breakfast food. I am very sorry that you cannot taste this, so I will taste it for you." Again, the audience laughed. "Now this is a combination and, by the way, one of the finest breakfast foods that you or anyone else has ever seen. It is a combination of the sweet potato and the peanut, and if you will pardon a little digression [turning away from the main subject being discussed] here I will state that the peanut and the sweet potato are twin brothers and cannot and should not be separated. They are two of the greatest products that God has ever given us. They can be made into a perfectly balanced ration. If all of the other foodstuffs were destroyed…a perfectly balanced ration…could be made with the sweet potato and the peanut.…

Another congressman could not resist the temptation to throw in a racial remark as he asked Carver, "Do you want a watermelon to go along with that?" Without pausing or showing irritation, Carver replied, "Well, of course, you do not have to have it. Of course, if you want a dessert, that comes in very well, but you know we can get along pretty well without dessert. The recent war has taught us that." That congressman made no further remarks.

Throughout his lecture, Carver's time was extended. At one point during the hearing, the chairman said, "Go ahead, brother. Your time is unlimited." When one congressman asked Carver, "Did you make all of these products yourself?" Carver replied, "Yes, Sir. They are made there in the research laboratory. That is what the research laboratory is for. The sweet potato products now number 107 up to date. I have not finished working with them yet. The peanut products are going to beat the sweet potato products by far. I have just begun with the peanut...."

As he was concluding his testimony, Carver noted that the committee had been shown only about half of the products he had made from the peanut. In less than an hour, Carver had successfully argued for the passage of a tariff to protect the interests of the American peanut industry. Carver had also cast himself in the role of a nationally famous scientist. He was to become known by citizens everywhere as "The Peanut Man" following coverage of his testimony in hundreds of newspapers.

Four months after the hearings in Washington, Carver addressed the delegates attending the United Peanut Growers' Association convention in Chicago. His topic was "The Potential Uses of the Peanut." In 1922 the Peanut Growers' Exchange covered the expenses of a Carver exhibit at the Greater Four County Fair in Suffolk, Virginia. The Suffolk Negro Business League provided Carver with housing and entertainment during his visit.

Carver was no longer engaged in most of the activities that had occupied his time during his first two decades at Tuskegee. His latest projects began to cast him in the role of "creative chemist." In 1922 the North Carolina Negro Farmers' Congress presented him with a silver loving cup for "Distinguished Scientific Research." Carver's role in the laboratory was beginning to overshadow his earlier role as an educator. Carver also began to emerge as a national folk hero. Articles about his life and discoveries began to appear frequently in newspapers and magazines.

Carver wished to spend more time in the laboratory and less time in the fields and classrooms at Tuskegee. This desire was based largely on his changing views of economic needs and answers. Early in his career Carver pushed for crop diversification. He emphasized the need for the southern farmer to abandon King Cotton. Carver had pushed for two major substitute crops: peanuts and sweet potatoes. Many farmers listened to Carver and began planting peanuts and sweet potatoes. This trend pleased Carver. Then one day he had a disturbing conversation with the widowed owner of a plantation. She had listened to Carver and planted peanuts. Her crop was successful. She then asked Carver what she could do with the peanuts. There were no buyers. Her peanuts were rotting in the fields.

The widow's plight and question bothered Carver. He realized he had not looked at the long-range situation. Carver believed the peanut and sweet potato were the crops needed to save the southern farmer. Now he would have to find a market for the crops. Such markets could result from the development of new industries that could use the crops for raw materials. As he began to search for answers, Carver retreated to his laboratory.

During his career Carver made approximately three hundred products from the peanut. He made ten beverages including blackberry punch, peanut lemon punch, and peanut beverage flakes. In the field of cosmetics, some of his products were antiseptic soap, baby massage cream, face cream, oil for hair and scalp, peanut oil shampoo, glycerine, and shaving cream. He produced about thirty dyes for cloth, nineteen dyes for leather, and assorted paints, as well as seventeen wood stains. Buttermilk, chili sauce, chop suey sauce, dry coffee, mayonnaise, mock goose, mock oyster, oleomargarine, vinegar, Worchestershire sauce, thirty-two types of milk, substitute asparagus, and ground white pepper made from the vines were some of the food products obtained from the peanut. Some of his medicinal products were a castoria substitute, a treatment for goiter, iron tonic, laxatives, a castor oil substitute, and tannic acid.

Carver used every part of the peanut in his creative experiments. He produced eleven types of wallboards from the hulls. He used the peanut skins and vines to produce an assortment of paper. Hulls were widely used in producing many animal feeds. Some additional products made from the peanut were axle grease, gasoline, glue, linoleum, nitroglycerin, printer's ink, plastics, rubber, wood filler, and sweeping compound.

Carver's other favorite crop substitute was the sweet potato. He used the sweet potato to produce at least 156 products. Some of the unexpected food products made from the sweet potato were substitute chocolate, ground coffee, egg yolk, lemon drops, tapioca, and vinegar. Some nonfood products made from the sweet potato were seventy-three dyes, library paste, synthetic cotton, synthetic silk, and ink.

By 1923 Carver was convinced that many of his products were ready to be marketed. Carver was not interested in the day-to-day work associated with operating a business. Throughout his career he had sought help from others such as Booker T. Washington and Emmett J. Scott in handling the applied or practical aspects of his work. In the early 1920s Carver hired Ernest Thompson as his business manager. He had known Thompson since 1913. Thompson's family was prominent in Tuskegee. Thompson wanted to form a company that would become a "lasting monument" to Carver and serve as a "benefit to mankind for years to come." Thompson's responsibilities included attracting both investors and manufacturers and helping to get patents.

In March 1923 Thompson made arrangements for an exhibit of Carver's products at the Cecil Hotel in Atlanta,

Georgia. A private railroad car was sent to Tuskegee to provide Carver's transportation and lodging during the exhibit.

The purpose of the exhibit was to attract potential investors. The exhibit proved very successful. On August 21, 1923, an application for the incorporation of the Carver Products Company was filed in Fulton County, Georgia. The function of the company was to be the "buying, selling and dealing in formulae and patented processes for the development of various and sundry products, such as food, dyes, stains, paints and other like products from the sweet potato, the peanut, the pecan, the okra, the dandelion, the black oak.... "The company was a type of holding company that was not to be involved in manufacturing. Other companies were to be sold the processes either directly or on a royalty (percentage of profit) basis. During its four years of existence the company obtained three patents. The patents covered two paint processes and one process for the making of cosmetics from clay and peanuts. The company failed because of a lack of money and time on the part of the company's officers.

One Carver product did reach the commercial market in the 1920s. In 1922 Carver formulated a compound called Penol. It was an emulsion (liquid suspension) of peanuts in creosote. Creosote, which is a liquid distilled from wood tar, was used at the time in medicines for bronchitis. Carver believed that the added peanuts would provide nutrition as well as help reduce the irritation and nausea associated with taking creosote as a medicine.

The Carver Penol Company was founded by Thompson and other investors around 1926. A pamphlet advertising Penol stated that the product "was composed of some of the best known and most proven remedies" for coughs, sore throat, bronchitis, catarrh, pulmonary, and stomach troubles. The product was described as being a "Tissue Builder, Intestinal Cleanser, Germ Arrester, Nerve Food and Intestinal Antiseptic." Although the brand name Phenol was protected by copyright, the product was not patented.

The product proved to be unprofitable for the original investors. Thompson realized he was not the person who could successfully market Penol. He began to seek others who were interested in marketing the product. On March 29, 1932, Thompson signed a contract with J. T. Hamlin, Jr., a businessman from Danville, Virginia, regarding the production and marketing of Penol. The contract gave Hamlin's company the right to produce and sell Penol for a monthly fee of $100 and a royalty of $2\frac{1}{2}$ cents per bottle. By July 1932 low sales volume led to a 50 percent reduction in the monthly fee. In spite of low sales volume, Hamlin was still hoping to be successful with this product as late as 1941. At that time he was still trying to get permission from Carver to use his picture on the Penol carton and in advertisements for the product. Eventually Hamlin stopped making Penol.

Throughout his career Carver failed to market any of his products successfully. Carver's diverse research interests contributed in large part to his failure in business. His interest shifted rapidly from one product to another. If Carver had concentrated his energy and time toward perfecting one or even a few products, he would have been more successful in the marketplace. However, the marketplace and profits were not of much interest to Carver. His lack of business skills was never used by the public in measuring his success and personal worth.

11

The Tree Bears Its Fruit

The public measured Carver's success by his many recognitions and social contributions. In 1923 his recognition by two very different groups served to illustrate his broad social appeal. During his exhibit at the Cecil Hotel in March, he received a letter of praise from a conservative group of southern women. The Atlanta chapter of the United Daughters of the Confederacy (UDC) sent him a letter expressing their interest in and appreciation of his work. On September 4, 1923, Carver was honored by the National Association for the Advancement of Colored People (NAACP). He traveled to Kansas City, Kansas, to receive the prestigious Spingarn Medal in recognition of his distinguished research in agricultural chemistry. The medal was presented to Carver by the attorney general of Kansas.

The Spingarn Medal had been established by Joel Elias Spingarn in 1914. Spingarn, a white publisher and former chair of the NAACP Board of Directors, established the medal to recognize the African Americans who were considered to have made the greatest contribution to the advancement of the race during the previous year.

Thus, within a few months Carver had been praised by both southern whites and the NAACP. The NAACP had been founded in 1909 by W. E. B. Du Bois and others. It did not follow the social style promoted by Booker T. Washington, that is, one of accommodating white society. Its leaders were actively involved in programs designed to challenge and change the rules of racial injustice. The NAACP leaders knew Carver's approach to racial issues was close to that held by Washington. Yet they believed his efforts proved him to be worthy of this award. Carver's tendency to avoid talking about racial issues most likely contributed to his being acceptable to racially divided groups. Carver held the view that each individual was a member of God's family. He believed that the passage of time would enable the two races to live in harmony. In the meantime, his research was intended to help all people of all races.

Carver was invited to visit and speak on many college campuses. In August 1920 he had been invited to visit Mississippi State College. The invitation to speak there was extended by the college president. The following two years included speeches at both Mississippi College in Clinton, Mississippi, and Clemson College in Clemson, South Carolina. These invitations, as well as warm receptions given by church audiences, led to Carver's being invited to attend a summer conference in Blue Ridge, North Carolina. The invitation was made in 1923. It was extended by both the Commission on Interracial Cooperation (CIC) and the Young Men's Christian Association (YMCA). The summer conferences had become an annual event designed to increase better racial relationships. Those attending the summer conference at Blue Ridge were white college students. When Dr. Robert Moton spoke before the group in 1920 he was warmly greeted by the students. However, he was housed and fed separately from the whites. Carver ran into the same restrictions. He accepted them graciously.

Carver's address before the group concerned the bountiful resources in nature and how they could be used to benefit everyone. Carver's remarks were followed by loud applause. Many of the students shook Carver's hand. One of the students most impressed by Carver was Jimmie Hardwick, who had been a captain of Virginia Polytechnic Institute's football team. Carver was impressed immediately by Hardwick's sincerity. He invited the young man to become one of "his boys." Carver explained that when he formed friendships with young people who were open to his message, he thought of them as his adopted children. Hardwick, a Virginian descendant of former slave owners, replied, "I'd like to be one of your boys, Professor Carver, if you will have me."

Hardwick became one of hundreds of young men who joined Carver's "adopted" family as he spoke at numerous colleges, religious meetings, and assorted conferences. The friendships established between Carver and "his boys" involved letter writing that lasted for years. Carver became a friend and mentor, or trusted guide, to hundreds of young men. The letters written by both Carver and "his boys" reveal feelings of deep emotion and affection. In his letters, Carver always encouraged the young men to do their best and to maintain their personal commitment to the Creator.

When Carver attended the Blue Ridge conference in 1924, he did not have to sleep in separate quarters. Howard Kester, a member of a delegation from Lynchburg, Virginia, invited Carver to share a cottage with the two dozen students in his delegation. Carver was still unable to eat in the dining hall. However, his "Virginia boys" took food to him. When it was announced that Carver would be speaking before everyone at the conference, delegations from Florida and Louisiana expressed their plans to walk out during his speech. When the moment of decision arrived, however, the walkout did not occur. Carver's personality won out over the feelings of racial hatred. After Carver had finished his speech, the leader of the Florida delegation stood and apologized for the planned walkout.

Carver was so popular among the students that he was invited to stay for several extra days. He was able to meet with the students on an individual basis. The demand for Carver was so great that someone was assigned to make appointments. The interviews were limited to fifteen minutes each. Carver was kept busy from four in the morning until midnight. He met with several delegations and was invited to visit many campuses. Four delegations begged him to stay with them in their cottages the following year. Later, some of the students would visit Carver at Tuskegee. That decision was very costly for Howard Kester. When he left to visit Carver, his father told him not to return home.

In 1924 Carver went to New York City. He had been invited to speak to the Women's Board of Domestic Missions of the Reformed Church in America. The meeting was held in the Marble Collegiate Church. During his lecture, Carver emphasized his reliance on God for inspiration as he conducted his research. He said, "No books ever go into my laboratory. I never have to grope for methods; the method is revealed at the moment I am inspired to create something new."

The audience seemed pleased by Carver's comments. A

reporter from the *New York Times* proved otherwise. He wrote an editorial entitled "Men of Science Never Talk That Way." In the editorial, Carver's lack of scientific spirit was criticized. The writer stated that real chemists do not scorn the use of books nor do they credit their successes to mere inspiration. He stated that such talk would bring ridicule to both Tuskegee Institute and the black race.

Carver was hurt deeply by the comments. On November 24, 1924, Carver wrote a letter to the editor of the *New York Times* defending both his religious beliefs and his public statements. Carver wrote, "I have read with much interest your editorial pertaining to [dealing with] myself in the issue of November 20th. I regret exceedingly that such a gross misunderstanding should arise as to what was meant by 'Divine inspiration.' Inspiration is never at variance [in disagreement] with information; in fact, the more information one has, the greater will be the inspiration." Carver listed his academic credentials. He named over fifty scientists whose works had inspired him. He noted that one can learn methodology, the rules and procedures, by studying a textbook. However, the master of analytical work no longer needs to refer to those books while conducting original research. With original research, the answers are not in books. Whenever one uses prior knowledge to plan experiments and to think of possible experimental approaches, that is "inspiration."

Carver never earned a doctorate. Yet he was addressed as "Doctor" throughout most of his career. On November 26, 1926, he wrote to Professor Louis Pammel:

The prefix "Dr." as attached to my name is a misnomer [use of a wrong title]. I have no such degree.

It was started fully 25 years ago, by a Mr. Daniel Smith.... He was greatly interested in my work, and said have you a Dr.'s degree, I said no. Well he said you ought to have it, your work really more than entitles you to it.

So from that time on he called me Dr. Others took up the refrain, he put it in the news-paper articles he wrote. I 'was powerless to stop it. I regret that such an appendage was tacked on but I cannot help it [original spelling and punctuation].

In 1928 Simpson College bestowed on Carver an honorary doctor of science degree. He could thereafter officially be addressed as "Doctor."

In addition to many other activities, Carver served as a consultant to the peanut industry from 1924 to 1938. He served the industry in many capacities. He was a technical adviser, lecturer, and writer for many of the industry's publications. In 1924 Tom Huston, founder of the Tom Huston Company in Columbus, Georgia, became a close friend of Carver. He often sought Carver's advice. In 1929 Huston asked Carver to join his research staff. Carver refused to leave Tuskegee but still offered to help Huston whenever his help was needed.

Huston was always trying to find some way to show his appreciation for Carver's help. Carver was still refusing to accept money for his advice. Huston was able to get Carver to accept some gifts such as a typewriter, a blanket, a gold peanut, and even a diamond ring. Later, Huston learned that Carver had added the ring to his mineral collection rather than wear it. In 1931 Huston commissioned Isabelle Schultz of Baltimore, Maryland, to sculpt a likeness of

Carver. It was then sent to Italy to be cast as a bronze bas-relief. He had two plaques made. One was hung in the laboratory of the Tom Huston Company. The other plaque was presented to Tuskegee Institute.

In the mid-1930s Carver not only helped Tom Huston but the entire peanut industry. Carver identified fungi that were destroying the peanut crops. His work with the problem was enough to bring the forces of the United States Department of Agriculture to address the situation. The agent sent to survey the extent of the fungal infestation was Paul R. Miller. During his two-year survey, he was greatly aided by Carver. Miller reported Carver's expertise in the field of mycology to the USDA. In recognition of Carver's expertise, the USDA named him a "collaborator" with the Plant Disease Survey in 1935.

Carver was in so much demand as a speaker throughout the country that Tuskegee Institute provided him with a traveling secretary. The secretary, Harry O. Abbott, was responsible for making arrangements for Carver's trips. He also accompanied Carver on the trips. In 1930 Abbott arranged for a fifteen-day tour through Kansas, Oklahoma, and Texas. During this tour Carver appeared before many different groups. He visited several schools, YMCA groups, civic organizations, and the Oklahoma State Teachers Association. In Austin, Texas, he was invited to address a joint session of the state legislature.

During this tour Carver once again was confronted by a reminder of racial injustice. Abbott made reservations for him and Carver to travel by train from Oklahoma City to Dallas, Texas. The arrangements were made by telephone. Abbott made Pullman sleeping car reservations with the Wichita agent of the Atchison, Topeka and Santa Fe Railway System. When the pair tried to board a Pullman car in

Oklahoma City, they were refused permission. They were forced to ride in a segregated coach that lacked special sleeping facilities.

The resulting bad publicity led to apologies by company officials. The president of the railway company sent his personal apology to Carver. Carver accepted the apology. He also voiced his approval of the company's pledge that in the future "every courtesy possible will be extended to colored patrons."

The Great Depression of the 1930s dealt a severe blow to Carver. He showed very little interest in money. He often would wait months before bothering to cash his paychecks. This inattention to cashing his checks presented problems for the college treasurer. The treasurer found it almost impossible to balance his books for the auditors. Whenever Carver bothered to cash his checks he simply deposited the money in banks. In early 1933 someone asked Carver if he knew that the banks had failed. He replied that he had heard the news. He noted that all of his money was deposited in three banks. Carver lost about $40,000 at that time. Regarding his loss he simply said, "I guess somebody found a use for the money. I wasn't using it."

Carver had neither the time nor energy to be sidetracked by financial concerns. In 1930 he had begun to address the problems associated with polio. He turned to the peanut for the answer. He believed that the peanut contained substances which were medicinal. To prove his theory he began to treat two polio victims with peanut oil and massage. By 1931 he began to give hints that he had discovered a new form of therapy for polio victims. In December 1933 an Associated Press writer, T. M. Davenport, traveled to Tuskegee to interview Carver. Davenport's article was published December 30, 1933. Carver was quoted as saying, "It has been given out that I have found a cure [for polio]. I have not, but it looks hopefully." Carver had noticed that peanut oil could be absorbed through the skin. This was brought to his attention after he had used it as a base in a skin lotion. He said, "I gave it to some ladies to use, and those inclined to be fat brought it back to me, saying they could not use it because it made them gain weight."

Davenport reported Carver's success with his two polio patients. Both patients were teenage boys. Carver noted that the peanut oil massages resulted in improved skin coloration and an increase in the size of the leg muscles. After nine therapy sessions one boy had been able to abandon his crutches for a cane. The second boy, who was less severely afflicted, had been able to return to playing football. Davenport reported that Carver had applied the oil and massage to 250 patients. Every patient had shown improvement. Carver had meant to say that he had used the therapy for many conditions. At the time he had only treated the two polio patients.

Davenport's article appeared in many newspapers. The following day many people traveled to Tuskegee to seek help. Carver received thousands of letters requesting information regarding his new therapeutic techniques. His advice led to a national shortage of peanuts throughout 1934 and 1935. Carver himself had great difficulty in securing peanut oil from distributors. By the summer of 1935, Carver began to stress the importance of massage in his proposed therapy. He came to realize any oil was suitable for treatment.

In September 1934 Carver had begun to massage the withered legs of Emmett Cox, Jr. This state employee had been stricken by polio at the age of two. Some twenty-two years later he was using braces when he met Carver. By March 1935 Cox had stopped using his braces and was regaining the use of his legs.

Franklin D. Roosevelt and George W. Carver.

As early as 1933 there was speculation that Carver was massaging the legs of President Franklin D. Roosevelt, who suffered from polio. Some supposed that Carver visited Roosevelt at the presidential retreat in Warm Springs, Georgia. In 1938 Carver mailed some peanut oil to the White House. The following year Roosevelt stopped by Tuskegee during a tour of the South. A photograph of Roosevelt shaking hands with Carver appeared in newspapers throughout the country. The following week Roosevelt wrote a letter to Carver. Roosevelt wrote, "I do use peanut oil from time to time and I am sure it helps."

In 1935 two changes occurred with respect to Carver's work situation. One was the appointment of Dr. Frederick D. Patterson as Tuskegee Institute's new president. Patterson, like Moton, was very supportive of Carver's every action. The other change involved Carter's meeting with Austin Wingate Curtis, Jr.

Curtis, a 1932 graduate of Cornell University, Ithaca, New York, was hired as an assistant to Carver. At the time he was offered the position with Carver, he was teaching at North Carolina Agricultural and Technical College, Greensboro, North Carolina. Curtis's hiring was made possible by a grant program. The grant was sponsored by the General Board of Education (GBE), a philanthropic organization. A grant is a gift of money given for a particular purpose. Part of the GBE grant provided for the "training of assistants to the personnel, who may be prepared to carry the work forward."

Carver had parted company with a few earlier assistants before Curtis appeared on campus in September 1935. When Curtis was escorted to Carver's door, Carver opened the door about twelve inches. He warmly greeted his new assistant through the partially opened door. He told Curtis that he was pleased to meet him and suggested that he look around campus and feel free to visit him if he had any questions. Shortly after Curtis had joined Carver, Carver wrote to Curtis's father. According to Carver, his new assistant "seems to me more like a son than a person who had just come to work for me." Until 1943 Curtis would serve Carver as both an assistant and son figure. There existed such a bond of friendship and devotion between the two researchers that Curtis was referred to as "Baby Carver."

Austin Wingate Curtis, Jr. (left), assisted Carver in his work.

Curtis became Carver's traveling companion, research assistant, and spokesperson.

Biographer Rackham Holt noted that Carver and Curtis enjoyed a very warm, cordial relationship. Curtis protected Carver from interruptions. He was always showing his concern for Carver's well-being. Carver was appreciative of Curtis's concern. Yet the aging scientist was always ready to show who was in charge of the situation. For example, when Curtis warned Carver about the dangers of standing in the cold without a coat, Carver replied, "It surprises me how I managed to live all these years without you. If you keep on aggravating me I shall lose my sweet disposition. Last night I lay awake worrying about you, tossing and turning for fully half a minute." Occasionally, Carver would remove his glasses and look at Curtis and say, "You don't suit me at all." To which Curtis would respond, "Sir, they say I grow more like Dr. Carver every day." Carver would challenge the comparison, "That's a fairy tale. You're enough to worry the horns off a mule." Carver would then hook his arm inside Curtis's arm and the two friends would go to investigate some project.

Carver was not the only individual concerned with experimenting with crops and soil. In Dearborn, Michigan, automotive industrialist Henry Ford had similar concerns. In 1929 Ford established the Edison Institute. It consisted of Henry Ford Museum and Greenfield Village. On the village grounds, he built both a chemical laboratory and a greenhouse in order to find "industrial uses for farm products." In 1931 the chemical plant experimented with extracting—that is, separating and obtaining—oil from orange peels and extracting furfural, a liquid aldehyde, from garbage. The workers also experimented with wheat, soybeans, and carrots. In another building, Dr. Edsel Ruddiman, Ford's boyhood schoolmate, was experimenting with wheat, soybeans, carrots, and tomatoes in attempting to "make milk without a cow." In 1932 Ford began to concentrate his farming efforts on the soybean. Elsewhere Ford had workers planting thousands of acres of soybeans. In a twenty-five-acre field at Greenfield Village, about five hundred experimental varieties of soybeans were grown. In 1932 the village chemical plant extracted soybean oil at the rate of six tons each day. The extracts were used to produce soybean bread, milk, butter, ice cream, and much of the material for an experimental plastic car.

In May 1935 Henry Ford hosted the First Dearborn Conference of the National Farm Chemurgic Council. (Chemurgy is the branch of science that applies chemistry to the industrial use of organic raw materials, especially from farm products.) This conference was attended by about three hundred agricultural chemists from all over the country. The group met in Ford's replica of Independence Hall. There they signed a "Declaration of Dependence Upon the Soil." When the group met in 1937, Carver was invited to speak. Ford visited with Carver while Carver stayed at the Dearborn Inn. This was the first meeting between the two men. Ford later entertained Carver at Greenfield Village. Carver gave a speech for the students of the Edison Institute.

Following his visit, Carver wrote to Ford, "Two of the greatest things that have ever come into my life have come this year. The first was the meeting of you, and to see the great educational project that you are carrying on...."

The year 1937 marked the beginning of a long series of honors bestowed upon Carver. Much of this was stimulated by the actions of Curtis and the officials at Tuskegee Institute. In the fall of 1936 they had begun to plan for a celebration of Carver's fortieth anniversary at Tuskegee. In

November a press release requested contributions of "not more than $1.00" to pay for the making of a bronze bust of Carver to commemorate the event. The bust was unveiled in a ceremony on June 2, 1937. The main address was presented by Dr. H. E. Barnard, Director of the Farm Chemurgic Council. He noted that Carver had begun to actively develop the science of chemurgy some forty years earlier. Carver's career was highlighted in articles in several newspapers and magazines, including *Time* and *Life*.

Other honors bestowed upon Carver in 1937 were honorary membership in the National Technical Association and the Mark Twain Society.

In March 1938 Henry Ford made his first visit to Tuskegee. He wanted to talk to Carver about some farming problems that had arisen on his plantation. Ford's plantation, Richmond Hill, was located in Ways, Georgia.

In April 1939 Ford's secretary Frank Campsall sent Carver some recent photographs of the Colored Community School which was under construction near Ways. Campsall explained, "It is planned that this will be a trade school, since it will not only give instruction in the usual grades, but will have in conjunction a woodworking and machine shop—also a small sawmill—where the students will have an opportunity to learn a practical trade." Campsall continued, "Mr. Ford has expressed a desire to let this school be known as the George Washington Carver School, provided you have no objection to his doing so." Later in 1939 Carver and Curtis visited Henry and Clara Ford at their plantation. On March 15, 1940, they returned for the dedication of the George Washington Carver School. Later Carver wrote, "I was with Mr. Ford the entire day. I don't think he left me fifteen minutes during the entire day. He rode with me in the car,

helped me over rough places, wouldn't let me walk any-
where, and kept the people away from me...."

In 1938 Carver's life story was featured in a Hollywood
movie. The film was shot on location in Tuskegee. It
featured several local persons. Booker T. Washington III
portrayed his grandfather. Carver played himself in his later
years. During the same year Carver was honored at the
Seventy-fifth Anniversary of Negro Progress held in Green-
ville, Mississippi. He was also presented with an Alumni
Merit Award by the Chicago Alumni Association of Iowa
State. The Phi Beta Sigma fraternity elected Carver to
membership in the Distinguished Service and presented him
with a Distinguished Service Key during a special service
conducted at Tuskegee.

In 1939 Carver's poor health forced him to limit both
his general activities and his travels. In April he was able to
attend a ceremony in Columbus, Georgia. The occasion
involved the Tom Huston Company presenting its bronze
bas-relief to an African-American high school in Columbus.
The same year included Carver's becoming the first African
American to address the *New York Herald-Tribune* Forum. He
was one of three recipients of Roosevelt Medals awarded by a
memorial society for President Theodore Roosevelt. He was
also elected to honorary membership in the American
Inventors Society.

Carver's last major tasks were intended to help preserve
his legacy and to insure a means by which his life's work
could be continued. During the Fortieth Anniversary celebration Curtis decided that Carver's work should be brought
together in one place for the sake of history. In 1938 the
officials at Tuskegee Institute designated the former campus
laundry building the George Washington Carver Museum.

The selection of a laundry facility to house Carver's lifelong collections and works seemed appropriate. The Carver Foundation was established to support the museum and to set up research fellowships for students.

As work on the facility began, Carver moved from Rockefeller Hall to Dorothy Hall, a guest house located near the laundry building. Thus, Carver was able to more easily supervise the work being done. In 1939 about 2,000 people attended the opening of the partially completed building. The hope of seeing the Carver Museum reach its full potential seemed to give new life to the ailing Carver. He became very active in supervising every aspect of the project.

In early March 1941 Henry and Clara Ford traveled to Tuskegee to dedicate the George Washington Carver Museum. They inscribed their names in a wet cement cornerstone. They also donated soybeans and some plastic car parts made from soybeans to be placed in the cornerstone. During that visit, Ford, without Carver's knowledge, ordered an elevator installed in Dorothy Hall to assist Carver in reaching his second-story apartment. In a letter written to Ford dated September 29, 1941, Carver wrote,

> This is the third week that I have been using the marvelous elevator you gave and installed for me. What it is doing for me cannot be expressed in words, but God...will show you that it is a *life saver*. This letter is written with my own hand, the first one completed in nearly two years. I rarely attempted to sign my name...the heart was so bad....I can walk 50% better than when you were here. The Great Creator will reward you, I cannot.

In the early 1940s Ford decided to have a replica of Carver's birthplace constructed in Greenfield Village. The

George W. Carver and Henry Ford pose for a photograph in Ford's Dearborn Nutrition Lab in 1942.

cabin was designed from details provided by Carver. Ford had logs from the forty-eight states in the Union at that time shipped to Dearborn for their inclusion in the cabin.

In March 1942 the Fords visited Carver in Tuskegee. They began to plan a trip for Carver to visit them in Dearborn. During the following months Curtis and Campsall exchanged letters regarding the trip. Ford suggested that the trip be made in August when "flies and mosquitoes are not numerous here." Curtis was notified of the progress on the cabin. He was also advised that Ford wanted Carver to dedicate a nutritional laboratory during the visit.

In a letter written to Ford in July 1941 Carver had made mention of *Sida spinosa*, a member of the milkweed family. Carver wrote: "I am very certain it contains rubber as nearly all milkweeds do." Carver and Curtis arrived in Dearborn in July 1942. Their arrival caused widespread speculation in the newspapers that Carver had come to advise Ford regarding a new source of rubber, a material important for the auto industry and for the defense industry.

The laboratory was dedicated by Carver on July 21. Weed sandwiches, prepared under Carver's supervision were served at the dedication ceremony. Sandwich spreads prepared in the laboratory were also featured. During this visit Carver was entertained royally for two weeks. His residence was the Dearborn Inn. During this period, he dedicated his birthplace cabin. He even slept in it one night. His other activities included his speaking at a chapel service at the Edison Institute. He also had lunch with the Fords at Fair Lane, their home in Dearborn. Carver spent the last two weeks of his visit as a consultant at the newly dedicated Nutritional Laboratory.

In September 1942 Ford was invited to become a trustee

Carver a few months before his death.

of the George Washington Carver Foundation. Ford accepted the invitation.

On December 22, 1942, the last letter from Carver was received at Dearborn. In the letter addressed to Campsall, Carver wrote,

> The pair of black shoes that were made from my last [shoes] by the shoe cobbler in Greenfield Village have arrived. I cannot tell you how much they are appreciated....If you have ever observed a little girl who has just received a bright and cheery new dress and seen her behave, you could get some idea of how I am behaving in my new shoes. Please remember me most graciously to the shoe cobbler and wish for him a very happy and pleasant Christmas. I wish for you and yours, and all my friends up there a most pleasant and joyous holiday season. I am looking forward to your coming down next spring as I have missed you since my art rooms have been installed.

At 7:30 P.M. on January 5, 1943, Dr. George Washington Carver died. At 7:55 P.M. Dr. Frederick D. Patterson sent a telegram to Henry Ford notifying him of Carver's death. Ford was unable to attend the funeral. However, he sent a representative to the funeral. A floral blanket sent by Ford and his son Edsel draped Carver's casket. In a public tribute to Carver, Henry Ford said, "Dr. Carver had the brain of a scientist and the heart of a saint." Tributes were sent to Tuskegee Institute from persons throughout the world expressing their sorrow accompanying Carver's death. President Franklin Roosevelt wrote, "The world of science has lost one of its most eminent figures and the race from which he sprang an outstanding member...The versatility of his genius and achievements in diverse branches of the arts and

The George Washington Carver Museum in Tuskegee, Alabama.

sciences were truly amazing. All mankind are the beneficiaries of his discoveries.... I count it a great privilege to have met Dr. Carver...."

Funeral services for Carver were held in the campus chapel January 8.

Carver was laid to rest near the grave of Booker T. Washington. The grave site is marked by a beautifully curved white stone seat. The grave is covered by a marble slab. The inscription reads:

George Washington Carver Died in Tuskegee, Alabama, January 5, 1943. A life that stood out as a gospel of self-sacrificing service. He could have added fortune to fame but caring for neither he found happiness and honor in being useful to the world. The center of his world was the South where he was born in slavery some

79 years ago and where he did his work as a creative scientist.

Carver's death occurred during a period of widespread recognition for the aging scientist. However, his death signaled neither an end to his personal contributions nor to the bestowing of honors by a grateful public. Carver left his entire estate amounting to over $60,000 to the George Washington Carver Foundation. In Washington, D.C., Congress passed legislation creating the George Washington Carver National Monument, Diamond, Missouri. This historic site is visited annually by thousands of tourists.

Since Carver's death, each decade has witnessed additional honors commemorating his achievements. The United States government further honored him by issuing both a postage stamp and a half-dollar showing his likeness. It also named a Polaris submarine in his honor.

Sunday, April 8, 1990, signaled Carver's induction into the National Inventors Hall of Fame, Akron, Ohio. Dr. Benjamin Franklin Payton, president of Tuskegee University, accepted the award. On this occasion, Carver and Dr. Percy L. Julian, an outstanding chemist, became the first African Americans to receive this honor.

Without a doubt, the nation will continue to seek ways to acknowledge the contributions of Dr. George Washington Carver—humanitarian, educator, and scientist.

Important Dates

About 1865 George Washington Carver is born in Diamond Grove, Missouri. The exact date of his birth is unknown.

1890 Carver enrolls at Simpson College located in Indianola, Iowa. He studies art with Etta Budd.

1891 Carver transfers to Iowa State College of Agriculture and Mechanical Arts located in Ames, Iowa.

1893 Carver's painting *Yucca and Cactus* receives honorable mention at the World's Columbian Exhibition in Chicago.

1894 Carver receives bachelor of science degree in agriculture from Iowa State College. He is the college's first African-American graduate; Carver begins working toward a master's degree at Iowa State. He joined the faculty at Iowa State.

1896 Carver receives a master of science degree in agriculture from Iowa State College; Carver begins his work at Tuskegee Normal and Industrial Institute in Tuskegee, Alabama. He is appointed director and instructor in scientific agriculture and dairy science. He is also named director of the agricultural Experiment Station.

1916 Carver is elected a Fellow of the Royal Society for the Encouragement of Arts, Manufacturers, and Commerce, London, England.

1921 Carver testifies before the House Ways and Means Committee, Washington, D.C.

1922 Carver is presented with a silver loving cup by the North Carolina Negro Farmers Congress for distinguished science research.

1923 Carver is awarded Spingarn Medal by the NAACP for distinguished service to science.

1928 Carver is granted an honorary doctor of science degree by Simpson College.

1931 The Tom Huston Peanut Company, Columbus, Georgia, presents a bronze plaque to Tuskegee Institute in recognition of Carver's contributions to the peanut industry.

1935 Carver is appointed Collaborator, Mycology and Plant Disease Survey, Bureau of Plant Industry, U.S. Department of Agriculture.

1937 Carver is awarded honorary membership in the Mark Twain Society. He addresses the Third Farm Chemurgic Council meeting in Dearborn, Michigan, as personal guest of Henry Ford; a bust of Carver is unveiled on campus in recognition of his forty years of scientific research.

1938 The film *Life of George Washington Carver* is made in Hollywood, California, by the Pete Smith Specialty Company.

1939 Carver receives the Roosevelt Medal for his outstanding contribution to southern agriculture.

1941 The George Washington Carver Museum is dedicated at Tuskegee by Henry and Clara Ford. Carver is granted an honorary doctor of science degree by the University of Rochester; he also receives an Award of Merit from the Variety Clubs of America.

1942 Carver is granted an honorary doctor of science degree by Selma University, Selma, Alabama. Henry Ford erects the George Washington Carver Cabin in Greenfield Village, Dearborn, Michigan.

1943 Carver dies on January 5 at Tuskegee Institute.

Bibliography

Books

* Adair, Gene. *George Washington Carver*. New York: Chelsea House Publishers, 1989.

Carty, Ed. *George Washington Carver in Indianola: A Tour Guide*. Indianola, Iowa: Warren County Historical Society, 1990.

* Coy, Harold. *The Real Book About George Washington Carver*. Garden City, New York: Garden City Books, 1951.

Elliott, Lawrence, *George Washington Carver: The Man Who Overcame*. Englewood Cliffs, New Jersey: Prentice-Hall, Inc., 1967.

* Graham, Shirley, and Lipscomb, George D. *Dr. George Washington Carver—Scientist*. New York: Julian Messner, Inc., 1944.

Harlan, Louis R., and Smock, Raymond, eds. *The Booker T. Washington Papers*. Urbana, Illinois: University of Illinois Press, 1980.

Holt, Rackham. *George Washington Carver: An American Biography*. Garden City, New York: Doubleday and Company, 1943, 1963.

Kremer, George R. *George Washington Carver in His Own Words.* Columbia, Missouri: University of Missouri Press, 1987.

Manber, David. *The Wizard of Tuskegee: The Life of George Washington Carver.* New York: Crowell-Collier Press, 1967.

McMurry, Linda O. *George Washington Carver: Scientist & Symbol.* New York: Oxford University Press, 1981.

Means, Florence Crannell. *Carvers' George, A Biography of George Washington Carver.* Cambridge, Massachusetts: The Riverside Press; Boston: Houghton Mifflin Co., 1952.

* Moore, Eva. *The Story of George Washington Carver.* New York: Scholastic, Inc., 1971.

Scipio, L. Albert, II. *Pre-War Days at Tuskegee. Historical Essays on Tuskegee Institute (1881–1943).* Silver Spring, Maryland: Roman Publications, 1987.

Thrasher, Max Bennett. *Tuskegee: Its Story and Its Work.* New York: Negro Universities Press, 1969. Originally published in 1901 by Small, Maynard & Co., Boston.

Washington, Booker T. *Up From Slavery.* New York: Airmont Publishing Co., Inc. 1967. The original text printed in 1901 is available from several publishers.

Articles and Papers

Bryan, Ford R. "A Prized Friendship: Henry Ford and George Washington Carver." *Henry Ford Museum and Greenfield Village Herald,* Vol. 12 (1983) pp. 90–95.

Cobbs, Nicolas Hamner. "The Night the Stars Fell on Alabama." *The Alabama Review,* Vol. 22, no. 2 (April 1969), pp. 147–57.

* Readers of the Pioneers in Change book *George Washington Carver* will find this book particularly readable.

Fishbein, Toby. "George Washington Carver." Iowa State University Archives, April 1976.

Fuller, Robert P. "The Early Life of George Washington Carver." George Washington Carver National Monument. Diamond, Missouri. November 26, 1957. Photocopy.

Index

ACKNOWLEDGMENTS:

A special debt of gratitude is extended to the following individuals, institutions, and organizations for their help in making this biography a reality: The staff at Tuskegee University, especially Archivist Dr. Daniel T. Williams; the staff at the George Washington Carver National Monument, especially Laura Illige; the staff at the George Washington Carver Museum, especially Tyrone Brandyburg; the staff at Henry Ford Museum & Greenfield Village, Dearborn, Michigan, especially Archivist Jeanine M. Head; Dr. William D. Barnard, Chair, Department of History, University of Alabama; Nettie R. Chappelle; Bettie and Wayne Gross; John Ohneck; Dr. Elysa Toler-Robinson; the staff at Simpson College, especially Cynthia Dyer; the staff at the Parks Library, Iowa State University of Science and Technology, especially Becky S. Jordan; the Warren County Historical Society, especially Ed and Lois Carty, Indianola, Iowa; the Miami County Historical Society, Paola, Kansas, the staff of the District Court of Ottawa County, Minneapolis, Kansas, especially Donna Steinbrock; and the staff of the Ottawa County Museum, Minneapolis, Kansas, especially Curator Letha Levering.

PHOTOGRAPH ACKNOWLEDGMENTS:

George Washington Carver National Monument, National Park Service, Diamond, Missouri: pp. 7, 19, 78; James M. Gray: pp. 4, 121; From the Collection of Henry Ford Museum & Greenfield Village: frontispiece, pp. 111, 117, 119; Iowa State University Library/Special Collections: pp. 63, 71; Iowa State University Library/University Archives: p. 58; Tuskegee University Archives: pp. 27, 45, 65, 75, 90, 109.

About the Author

James Marion Gray was born in Fort McClellan, Alabama. He holds several degrees from Wayne State University, Detroit, Michigan. His academic degrees include a master of science and a doctor of philosophy degree. Most of his studies have been in the area of the biological sciences, especially microbiology and bacteriology. He is currently completing coursework in a degree program leading to a doctorate in higher education. Gray is a biology teacher at Lincoln Park High School, Lincoln Park, Michigan. He holds membership in several professional organizations. Some of his hobbies include photography, horticulture, and stamp collecting.